EUROPE'S SOCIAL INTEGRATION

The Foundation for European Progressive Studies (FEPS) is the think tank of the progressive political family at EU level. Our mission is to develop innovative research, policy advice, training and debates to inspire and inform progressive politics and policies across Europe. We operate as hub for thinking to facilitate the emergence of progressive answers to the challenges that Europe faces today.

FEPS works in close partnership with its members and partners, forging connections and boosting coherence among stakeholders from the world of politics, academia and civil society at local, regional, national, European and global levels.

Today FEPS benefits from a solid network of 68 member organizations. Among these, 43 are full members, 20 have observer status and 5 are ex-officio members. In addition to this network of organisations that are active in the promotion of progressive values, FEPS also has an extensive network of partners, including renowned universities, scholars, policymakers and activists.

Our ambition is to undertake intellectual reflection for the benefit of the progressive movement, and to promote the founding principles of the EU – freedom, equality, solidarity, democracy, respect of human rights, fundamental freedoms and human dignity, and respect of the rule of law.

Europe's Social Integration

WELFARE MODELS AND ECONOMIC TRANSFORMATIONS

By **László Andor**

Translated from Hungarian by **Stephen Anthony**

FEPS
FOUNDATION FOR EUROPEAN
PROGRESSIVE STUDIES

Published by London Publishing Partnership
www.londonpublishingpartnership.co.uk

Published in association with the Foundation for
European Progressive Studies
www.feps-europe.eu
European Political Foundation – N° 4 BE 896.230.213

Published with the financial support of the
European Parliament. The views expressed in this
report are solely those of the authors and do not
necessarily reflect the views of the European Parliament.

European Parliament

ISBN: 978-1-913019-67-9 (pbk)
ISBN: 978-1-913019-68-6 (ePDF)
ISBN: 978-1-913019-69-3 (ePUB)

A catalogue record for this book is available
from the British Library

Typeset in Adobe Garamond Pro by
T&T Productions Ltd, London
www.tandtproductions.com

Contents

Preface

The concept of the European social model has become unavoidable in the spheres of sociology and political economy since the beginning of the 1990s. Why the early 1990s? When exploring the genesis of the concept, this period must be highlighted for at least three reasons.

Firstly, most people historically associated Western European social models built on increasing prosperity and class compromise with post-war reconstruction and the Cold War period, but with the passing of the Cold War the political pillars of these social models shifted and the future of the welfare compromise became uncertain. Secondly, the acceleration of the process of European integration, the introduction of the single market and single currency, and the transformation of the Economic Community into a Union could not have occurred without the definition of the bloc's social dimension. The promise of a 'social Europe' found wide support, giving birth to initiatives at the European level that were immensely diverse in their character and strength. Thirdly, it was in precisely this period – specifically in 1990 – that the Danish sociologist Gøsta Esping-Andersen's published his landmark work on the models of welfare capitalism, which thereafter became an indispensable point of reference and resource, providing direction and inspiration to researchers in sociology and political economy alike.

Although the concept of the European social model is thus essentially contemporaneous with the inception of the EU, the three decades that have since elapsed have also been shadowed throughout by the debate over the relationship between European integration and the continent's social models. European integration remains sufficiently opaque and ambiguous for most observers to be unable to easily determine whether the EU is a protector of the welfare systems and social cohesion of member states or whether it is just another factor in a long list of threats.

Treatises on the sustainability of the welfare state, when dissecting the real or perceived causes and processes of its weakening, routinely point to the impact of demographic and technological changes, as well as the challenges posed by globalization and the ecological crisis. It is often very difficult to distinguish between what occurs as a consequence of political decisions and what is part of an independently prevalent megatrend. But though their causes may be unclear, it is an easier task to determine whether trends are improving or harming the societies they affect, thanks to the significant advance and relatively uniform propagation of social indicators.

One of the main players in the development of a uniform methodology is the EU itself. However, the extent to which the EU is able to – or even wishes to – protect, strengthen and develop the welfare systems of member states in accordance with its economic aspirations and its specific form of integration has been an absolutely justified topic of debate over the past ten to fifteen years. This volume – incorporating my previously published writings, of varying levels of detail – may be regarded as a product of such debates.

The outline of the present volume took shape in 2016 – at the time, without the specific intention of serving as the basis for a book – at a conference held in Paris to mark the sixtieth anniversary of the formation of the Council of Europe Development Bank. The panel on which I spoke was convened to address the challenges of European economic and social models. My brief contribution outlined the four factors that seemed the most critical at that moment from the perspective of the sustainability of welfare models: globalization, monetary integration, eastward enlargement and the dawn of the new digital era.

The book's first edition, published in Hungarian in 2017, relied on the above-mentioned contribution in exploring the relationship between welfare models and European crises, reviewing a quarter of a century of debate over the welfare state and emphasizing the East-Central European, and particularly the Hungarian, aspects of the issue. In discussing the four key challenges, I also saw it as important to examine the attempted responses, ideas and searches for solutions of various governments.

Readers of this English-language edition should also be aware that the question of the welfare state was one of the cardinal problems of social theory concerned with the change of political system in East-Central Europe at the end of the twentieth century. In the 1980s, at a time of chronic financial crisis and economic stagnation in state-socialist systems, it seemed to many that a welfare capitalist alternative existed for the countries of the region: that radical reforms leading towards a market economy might result in the adoption of the Finnish or Austrian models.

Ostensibly, there was no reason to doubt the feasibility of the welfare capitalist model during the period of regime change. The question of whether such an alternative existed at all did not need to be raised before the wider public in 1989–90, since the answer was *a priori* in the affirmative. Since then, though, the early illusions have been replaced by experience and a much more complex theoretical understanding of the capitalist system and its diverse variants.

Research into welfare capitalism is, therefore, at once a theoretical problem and a practical one closely related to the story of regime change and the questions it poses. How much did the promise of welfare capitalism influence the political forces involved in regime change at the end of the 1980s and into the ensuing decade? What criteria would serve as the basis for judging whether the East-Central European capitalism that came into being in the wake of the transformation of the 1990s was even of the welfare variety?

Moving into the twenty-first century, the questions of the 1990s needed to be supplemented with additional ones. Has capitalism in the west (and in the EU within it) become progressively more welfare-oriented, or are social reforms in the process of being reversed? To what extent can the Western European welfare model be regarded as an evolutionary target in today's capitalism, looked at as a pattern to follow elsewhere in the world? Does it help create a better society if the EU centralizes more powers in the field of social policy? And how have changes in this sphere impacted the programme of the most significant progressive tendency in Europe: social democracy?

It is impossible to provide exhaustive answers to all these questions in a single volume. However, what must be stated clearly is that the social reform of capitalism (whichever model is concerned) and the resilience of welfare systems continue to be crucial questions for politics and policy in Europe. New developments and challenges such as the digital revolution, successive waves of immigration and the currency union crisis do not replace but rather add nuance to and expand on such questions as the long-term sustainability of welfare institutions and the curbing of income inequalities.

The book's 2019 Italian edition offered a deeper analysis of the link between European social crises and populism – a link that appeared as a shared concern for Hungary and Italy, even if the origin of this concern was not exactly the same for the two countries. For Hungary, the autocratic degeneration of the political system was a combined product of the failed post-communist transition and the global financial crisis of 2008–9; for Italy, it was the eurozone crisis that triggered the collapse of support for traditional centre-left and centre-right parties and gave rise to new patterns of populism as well as hard-right nationalism.

The 2022 English-language edition has been prepared with a substantial reworking and expansion of the original text. Besides more detailed analysis of the original four problem areas, separate chapters are devoted to reconstruction of the EU's social dimension following the financial crisis as well as the impact of the Covid-19 crisis on social integration and European solidarity.

The unaltered goal of this enlarged new edition is to urge social scientists committed to the topic to engage in a collaborative exchange of thought and debate, particularly with respect to the connection between social models and European integration. Without questioning, and indeed by emphasizing, that Europe's welfare models are inherently to be understood within national or smaller regional frameworks, I argue that the prevailing trend – as a consequence of shared global challenges and ever-deepening European economic integration – nevertheless points towards a progressively stronger role to be assigned to the frameworks created by the EU.

This volume also provides additional economic and social statistics in reviewing the development of European social policy over the past three decades, and it discusses the guiding ideas that have determined the progress of welfare policy over this period. I trace the evolution of the EU's social dimension, looking at how social conditions in European countries developed during a period of major financial and economic crises. I also compare the progress of the principal welfare indicators in various individual regions.

Focusing on four key challenges, this book aims to highlight the objective, rather than the subjective, factors that threaten Europe's social models. At the same time, I will also stress that policy decisions do influence economic transformations, and in particular the collective response to crises, which is why the word 'megatrend' will be avoided as much as possible, whether regarding globalization or technological change.

With some qualification, I will acknowledge the post-World War II growth period as the 'golden age' of Western European and North American welfare states, without assuming that any kind of nostalgia would be a good guide either to understanding the key social questions of our time or to shaping progressive welfare policy. The clock cannot be wound back. One of the fundamental transformations guiding social policy and the thinking around it in new directions is precisely the ever closer economic integration of Europe.

The move from an Economic Community to a Union was bound to be connected with ambitions for the EU's social dimension and with the rise of the sometimes-elusive concept of the European social model. But for too long there was little understanding of the implications of the incomplete realization of the EU social agenda and the inconsistency between the ambition in this field and the architecture of economic governance. Indeed, this problem drove the EU into a situation in which the specific trajectory of macroeconomic governance became a threat to national welfare systems, and in turn the social crises in specific EU member states (and those of the eurozone periphery in particular) started to undermine confidence in EU integration as such.

The combination of objective challenges and hostile policies has become a mortal threat to social cohesion in Europe, giving rise to a generation of literature thematizing the fall, or near death, of European welfare states and the ideal of social Europe. While it will hopefully add further details and observations to the analysis of crises, this book is certainly not about lengthening the list of obituaries of the European social model, not least because in the decade following the crises of the 2000s the EU has indeed evolved to a new stage, drawing conclusions from policy failure, creating a new epistemic framework and responding to the most recent major test – the Covid-19 pandemic – with a much higher degree of solidarity than was the case for previous shocks.

In presenting the period between 2010 and 2014, I naturally draw on my own practical policy experience, accepting that in such cases more careful judgement is required for the observance of professional objectivity. On the other hand, the understanding of policy dynamics and the insights from first-hand expertise within EU institutions represent a privileged position for assessing the potential of the EU to contribute to the maintenance, further development and convergence of the social models of European nations.

My initial studies (and numerous subsequent writings) owe a great deal to material that I have read in Hungarian, which rightly remains in the list of references. The present work largely relies on contemporary literature on the topic, especially on English-language sources, chief among the latter being studies that discuss the correlations and interactions between economic processes and social developments, with a crucial focus on employment and welfare systems.

University courses over the period following 2014 assisted greatly in the systematic arrangement of the literature and the relevant policy experiences, primarily those run at Corvinus University of Budapest, ULB in Brussels, Berlin's Hertie School, Sciences Po in Paris and the European University Viadrina in Frankfurt (Oder), not forgetting lectures delivered at the College of Europe (Bruges), the European University Institute (Florence) and Cornell University (Ithaca, NY). The author dedicates this book to colleagues and students at the above-mentioned universities.

The rise and evolution of welfare states

THE ERA OF SOCIAL REFORMS

The institutions of welfare capitalism largely evolved in the period following the Great Depression of the 1930s and World War II.[1] This historical origin served as the basis for early theorists of the welfare state – principally T. H. Marshall[2] – to advance the theory of accumulatively achieved citizenship. According to Marshall (1949), the original eighteenth-century interpretation of citizenship was limited to basic civil freedoms (property ownership, the right of association, freedom of religion, etc.), to which political rights were attached in the nineteenth century, followed by social rights in the twentieth century.

The Great Transformation (1944), the principle work of Karl Polanyi,[3] took a somewhat different, fundamentally economically centred approach. Polanyi argued that, to a certain degree, social policy as a defence against exposure to markets – at the minimum level necessary for political stability – was not a later concomitant factor but rather a precondition for the development of a capitalist economy and society, both in England (his main case study) and elsewhere.

---

1   Useful reading in Hungarian for those interested in the origins, history and ideology of the welfare state includes works by Szamuely (1985), Tomka (2008), Ferge and Lévai (1991) and Nyilas (2009).

2   Thomas Humphrey Marshall, who taught at the London School of Economics, introduced the concept of social rights in his work *Citizenship and Social Class*, published in 1950. Later he headed the department of social sciences at UNESCO.

3   Karl Polanyi (Polányi Károly) was born in Vienna and grew up in Budapest. He obtained his PhD in Cluj (Kolozsvár), but was forced to emigrate following the revolutions of 1918–19. He subsequently lived in Austria, England and Canada, writing works on economics, anthropology and sociology; from 1947, he worked as a professor at Columbia University in New York.

Nevertheless, the welfare state emerged – in Polanyi's interpretation – not so much as an extension of nineteenth-century civilization than as a breaking away from it. As faith in the self-regulating market evaporated – accompanied by the collapse of the gold-based monetary system the gold standard and the unravelling of the peace in Europe that had been built on the balance of power – transition to a new era became necessary. Essentially this meant that economic processes that had become detached from their social foundations would be re-embedded in society, necessitating a stronger presence of redistribution and reciprocity as organizing principles.

Addressing the question of why there was an increasing tendency towards social welfare activity in capitalist states in every region following World War II, an examination of the specific historical circumstances may provide an answer. The global economic crisis of the 1930s shook the societies of Western Europe and North America, while World War II brought fresh ordeals and historic tragedies. Surviving the war and succeeding in the subsequent reconstruction necessitated a rebinding of the ties of social solidarity; national unity demanded new compromises among social classes. Reforms therefore needed above all to lay the foundations for a politically sustainable and functioning capitalist system.

A rethinking of social conditions was also necessary because of the example of the Soviet Union, as the momentum of its industrialization (together with the relative success of its fight against material deprivation and illiteracy) provoked, for a time, strong sympathy for communism among a broad segment of the working class – and a narrower segment of the intelligentsia – in the west. For leading politicians in Western Europe and North America, it became clear that post-war reconstruction could not mean a return to the previous model. Long before the end of the war, recognition of this fact was reflected in the most important document of British welfare policy: the Beveridge Report, published in 1942.[4] Although commissioned by the coalition

---

[4]   The original title of the report was *Social Insurance and Allied Services*; its author, William Beveridge, was a professor at the London School of Economics. The report proposed the incorporation of the various branches and elements of social care into a unified system.

government led by Winston Churchill, a Conservative, the document later served as a starting point for the establishment of free healthcare as a civil right, providing a guiding principle of social policy to the Labour government that entered office in 1945.

Besides William Beveridge, the Cambridge economist John Maynard Keynes was another intellectual architect of post-war welfare capitalism. The economic policy recommendations derived from his work focused on the enhanced role of the state and the central budget in the interest of maintaining full employment, ensuring effective demand for goods and services and, by those means, achieving steady economic growth (i.e. growth devoid of major cyclical fluctuations). Keynes made his name, both at home and abroad, with his analysis of the 1919 Versailles peace negotiations, as well as with his later critique of conservative economic policy. The macroeconomic concepts he would go on to present in his *General Theory*, published in 1936, appeared to be consistent with the principles and institutions of social redistribution subsequently proposed by Beveridge.

In the course of the twentieth century, every political tendency played a role in the development and reform of welfare models, but the effectiveness of these models and their capacity for renewal depended mainly on progressive politics – and, in Europe, primarily on the strength of social democracy. The programme of twentieth-century social democracy called for the social reform of capitalism, and the concept of the welfare state in the middle of the twentieth century carried the promise of substantial reform. Wherever a strong social democratic party did not (yet) exist, the struggles of organized labour, gathered into trade unions, account for the steps taken towards establishing social rights and safety nets.

Although Western European social democracy regarded all forms of the welfare state as part of its own programme, in reality it played a defining role in the formation of only the British and Scandinavian models. In Scandinavia in particular, reforms were regarded as steps on the path towards socialism, which was hardly the direction taken by many social reformers in the rest of the world, such as William Gladstone, Otto von Bismarck, Franklin D. Roosevelt or Ludwig Erhard, or indeed by Keynes and Beveridge, who were both liberal members of the House of Lords.

In the mid twentieth century, despite ideological differences, the consensus that formed regarding minimum social provision contributed to the creation of a unified concept of the capitalist centre. This included the criteria of freedom (in contrast to 'communist' systems), a potentially indefinite continuation of regained prosperity and the ability of state redistribution to create conditions of general material affluence wherever market competition served to accumulate the requisite wealth but a political adjustment was required to distribute those assets more evenly.

ECONOMIC PERFORMANCE AND SOCIAL WELFARE

The welfare models that evolved after World War II may have differed depending on which political tendency played the primary role in their development and on which national subsystem the equalizing effect of state intervention had the greatest impact (education, healthcare, taxation, etc.). What is clear, however, is that when we speak of a welfare state in that period we mean the development of some kind of 'mixed economy' (a capitalist system with significant government regulation or operating with some degree of public ownership) and that state distribution far surpassed nineteenth-century levels. For some countries in Europe not long after the war, this involved public spending that equalled as much as 35% of GDP, and even more thereafter (mainly but not exclusively in Scandinavia).

It is important to emphasize that the consolidation of Western European welfare models occurred during the reconstruction and quarter-century-long boom period following World War II. The sense of prosperity and improving material conditions was thus primarily created by reconstruction itself. At the same time, consistent income redistribution enabled broad layers of society to benefit from economic growth and allowed more and more forms of state provision to be established. Economists frequently refer to this period as a 'golden age', and sociologists talk of a period of evolution of the consumer society. In western democracies, the creation of income conditions facilitating mass consumption enabled a return to mass production. In light of experience – and Keynesian theory – it had been evident for a long time by the mid twentieth century that maintaining economic equilibrium and social stability was only possible with extensive state intervention and the regulation of investment and incomes.

At the same time, this economic golden age in Western Europe could not have come about without the powerful assistance of the United States, and specifically the Marshall Plan. This helped Europeans via substantial transfers of funds, simultaneously incentivizing them to view the reforms of the New Deal as a guiding light. France and the Netherlands elevated macroeconomic planning to the institutional level. In the United Kingdom the spirit of the post-war golden age was neatly encapsulated in Prime Minister Harold Macmillan's slogan that the British people 'have never had it so good'.[5] The sense of stability and material gain did not mean that periods of decline (recession) did not occur in the economy; rather, it meant that in the 1960s unemployment was no longer a concern – and inflation was not yet a worry – for governments or for the large majority of society.

Thanks to its rapid reconstruction during the post-war period, the notion of an 'economic miracle' became attached to West Germany. The story begins with the successful currency reform that followed the formation of the country in 1949. In the 1950s, West Germany was producing annual average economic growth of more than 8%, as a result of which unemployment decreased from 1.9 million to 200,000 over the decade. Average earnings in industry grew by 250% between 1950 and 1962, facilitating a truly continuous increase in the standard of living. The creators of the new model dubbed it the 'social market economy'. Its theoretical foundations could be traced back to the period preceding World War II, being primarily associated with Wilhelm Röpke and Alfred Müller-Armack, who acted as the inspiration for the economic and social policies pursued over two decades by the Christian Democrat government of West Germany under Konrad Adenauer and Ludwig Erhard. Although the German proponents of the social market economy thought in terms

---

5   Macmillan first used this famous phrase in front of his Conservative political colleagues in 1957. He himself adopted it from America's Democrats, who declared in their 1952 election campaign, 'You never had it so good.'

of a mixed economy, they nevertheless opposed Keynes's doctrine of regulated demand. In their view, the state needed to correct the market through regulation, so the German framework opened the way for the establishment of 'industrial democracy', which – in contrast to the British model – assumed an intensive 'social partnership' between employers and employees.

From the ownership perspective, post-war nationalization signified an important step in the transition to mixed economies in Western Europe, particularly in network industries that functioned as natural monopolies (energy, transport, communications), but often also at strategic points in heavy industry and in the banking system. Besides private and public ownership, the social economy was also strong in certain countries (such as France and Italy), meaning the reaffirmation and (re)integration of social considerations into economic organizations, facilitated principally through cooperative ownership. In many countries (such as the United Kingdom), a great many social enterprises and charitable investment funds operated for both economic and social benefit, funded by donations both large and small.

The political goal of reducing the instability, unemployment and growing inequality and poverty that are inherent to an economy based on private capital can only be achieved through progressive economic and social policy. The functioning of the economy (through both boom and bust) always has an impact on the social policy agenda. It can delineate the framework of social policy while simultaneously setting its tasks. If the economy is functioning poorly and economic policy is proving ineffective, then the number of tasks for social policy will be greater but the funding at its disposal will be depleted. When using indexes to characterize the performance of a country's welfare system, therefore, such indicators generally take into account the combined impact of social policy and the economy.

At the same time, economic performance is not the only precondition for the successful operation of a welfare system: the relationship also works in reverse. It is for precisely this reason that David Garland (2016) emphasizes the necessity and universality of the formation of welfare states under the capitalist system when he asserts that 'the welfare state should be viewed not as a moment in post-war history, a radical left-wing politics, a questionable handout to the poor, or a drag on the economy, but instead as a fundamental aspect of modern government – universally present in all advanced societies in one form or another – that operates as an indispensable means of making capitalist economies socially and economically sustainable'. It is nevertheless important to add that the generalization refers not to capitalism in general, but rather to the democratic species of capitalist systems. As Garland (2016, p. 3) states: 'Among social scientists, the normality and functional necessity of welfare states in capitalist democracies is a settled empirical claim.'

It follows that, insofar as the welfare state evolved as the 'immune system' of capitalism (as the American economist Lester C. Thurow put it), we should not be surprised that in discovering the 'diseases' that endanger its functioning, this immune system has become increasingly complex and wide-ranging. The welfare system as broadly understood has come to encompass the regulation of working conditions, provision for the unemployed, the pension and healthcare systems, housing policy, education and child care, as well as the income redistribution required to finance all these components.

WELFARE CAPITALISM AND ITS VARIANTS

For a long time, the welfare state proved a rather elastic concept; like the concept of democracy itself, it was used in political discourse to denote systems established in a variety of ways. A new chapter in the scholarly analysis of the welfare state opened in the 1990s, when the work of Denmark's Gøsta Esping-Andersen (1990) convincingly presented the differences between the various types of welfare capitalism. The exploration of variant models provided impetus for the examination of the various systems' origins for all those wishing to understand contemporary changes and realistic alternatives.

The first and most important distinction to make with regard to individual programmes is whether the various forms of social provision are granted to beneficiaries on a universal basis or selectively (that is, whether the assessment of who is – or is not – entitled to benefits falls within the remit of an institution set up for this purpose). The third possibility is that entitlement to social provision comes about by means of an insurance contract (meaning that for a person to become a beneficiary their prior contribution to financing the system is required). A similar classification criterion is the extent to which the state takes on the role of social provision: whether it merely regulates, finances as well, or actually performs the role itself through its own apparatus. Based on these criteria, it can be determined how far a given system has moved away from covering fundamental needs through the market, and to what extent it has moved closer to the other pole: of politically recognizing and ensuring entitlement. Changes in the functioning of the welfare state, both historically and in the present, can mainly be characterized in terms of the direction and extent of shifts between these two poles.

Based on Esping-Andersen's classic work, three basic types of welfare capitalism can be distinguished (see Table 1): the modern liberal model, a typical example being the United States; the social democratic model, the best-known example being Sweden; and the corporatist model, of which the most characteristic example is Germany.

Comparing the three basic models and their respective examples, we see that the earliest comprehensive social policy measures were introduced in Germany in the 1880s under the government of Otto von Bismarck.[6] Pressure from the social democratic labour movement played a part in this. In the political sense, Bismarck's goal was precisely to disarm and cut off this opposition (aiming to show that the powers-that-be were at least as much the friend of the workers as were the socialists). From the perspective of economic policy, the introduction of health, accident and pension insurance was aimed at arresting the emigration of German workers to America – an aim that met with success at the time. Following World War II, the Christian Democrats proclaimed the socialization of the market economy in West Germany, and with this the welfare state, construed as a synonym for social policy, became an organic part of the social system, preserving the dominance of the insurance principle.

---

6   Otto von Bismarck served as minister president of Prussia and chancellor of the German empire between 1862 and 1890. His social laws were passed in the 1880s: sickness insurance in 1883, accident insurance in 1884 and pension insurance (old age and disability) in 1889.

Table 1. Variants of welfare capitalism (after Gøsta Esping-Andersen).

	Poverty/ inequality	Employment	Gender	Social insurance
Social democratic	Low	Generally high level of employment and low unemploy-ment	Child care facilitating high employment among women	Redistribu-tive
Corporatist	Medium	Lower level of employ-ment, higher unemploy-ment	Low employ-ment among women, incentives to stay at home	Income-based
Liberal	High	High level of employment, low unem-ployment	Many women working part time, a lack of child care	Means-tested (more recently with workplace benefits)

In the United States, welfare programmes were introduced under the aegis of Franklin D. Roosevelt's liberal Democratic Party in response to and during the Great Depression of the 1930s. As governor of New York, Roosevelt had already displayed conspicuous activism at the outbreak of the global crisis, and as president he reformed American capitalism within the space of a few years. His New Deal agenda began with the renewed regulation of the financial system and continued with public works programmes. The second phase of the New Deal saw the organization of unemployment insurance at the federal level (in 1935). The American welfare state, born in the midst of a social and political emergency, can be characterized as an inorganic addition to the capitalist system. The Democratic Party continued to preserve the spirit of the New Deal for decades, and even attempted to develop it further in the 1960s.[7]

---

7   President Lyndon B. Johnson declared his war on poverty in 1964 under the slogan of the 'Great Society', but it became gradually pushed into the background of the political agenda.

The welfare state in Sweden – with antecedents dating back to the 1930s[8] – developed in the period following World War II and entailed a far greater role for trade unions and local government compared with the models of Germany and the United States. The long-lasting hegemony of the Social Democrats enabled state planning activity to be extended to all sectors of the economy and social provision to be covered by taxes. As a consequence, political and social considerations permeated the entire economy, so that in Scandinavia the term 'welfare state' came to be understood as a synonym for the social and economic system as a whole (and not merely as a subsystem thereof).

As a consequence of the decommodification[9] of labour, the radical elimination of conflicts in society and the introduction of wide-reaching social partnership and care, the Swedish model was regarded for a very long time as the social model of the future in other western countries, where progressive forces believed they saw their own path forward revealed in it. And yet, of the Western European and North American systems, it was the Swedish model that moved furthest away from the fulfilment of fundamental needs via market means, and which in the 1970s would go on to experiment with further solutions towards the complete socialization of the economy and social policy and the still more vigorous politicization of economic management. The Swedish model emerged as the champion in terms of women's employment levels and ascent to leading positions, while among the member states of the Organisation for

---

8   In Sweden, the Saltsjöbaden Agreement of 1938 laid the foundations of labour relations and the welfare state. From this time on, dialogue and cooperation between employers, employees and the state could be counted on as the most important guiding principle of society.

9   For Esping-Andersen, decommodification means that the welfare state promotes citizens' lives (income distribution as well as a wide range of public services) largely as independent of market mechanisms. Various services are regarded by citizens as social entitlements rather than commodities that must be paid for, so that the market economy does not transform into a market society. To measure this impact, Esping-Andersen defined a 'decommodification index'.

Economic Co-operation and Development (OECD),[10] the United States languishes to this day at the bottom of the ranking with respect to the length of paid maternity leave.

THE END OF CONSENSUS: ATTACKS FROM THE RIGHT

Despite the evolution of differing models, the quarter-century following World War II saw the emergence of a kind of welfare consensus, which held that the functioning of capitalism needed to be reconciled with more general democratic and social norms through the incorporation of certain corrective mechanisms. In time, however, criticisms of this welfare consensus would emerge from both the left and the right of the political spectrum.

The thinking of the New Left – which had a great influence, for example, on the student movements of the late 1960s – asserted that welfare benefits essentially meant only that certain strata of society that enjoyed a comparatively favourable bargaining position were 'paid off' to ensure that the oppressive structures of capitalism were further maintained, and that a significant portion of state benefits were enjoyed by those belonging to powerful interest groups – indeed, in some cases specifically by the rich. Eventually, they argued, those relying on social benefits become dependent on the bureaucracies that manage welfare systems and – particularly in the liberal model – end up losing their entire independent material means and taking on the stigma of poverty in order to qualify as deserving of support. The welfare state also came in for criticism for its nationalist and protectionist character, as if redistribution were an attempt to offset the discriminatory impacts of the market exclusively within national boundaries while solidarity for the poor and vulnerable remained entirely absent on the international stage. A programme of economic emancipation for women was also lacking, while in many cases ethnic and other minorities found themselves left outside the protective

---

10   The OECD, with its headquarters in Paris, groups together the most advanced market economies. Its predecessor, the administrator of the Marshall Plan, was the Organisation for European Economic Co-operation (OEEC).

ramparts of the welfare state. In German sociology – and elsewhere in its wake – the concept of the 'two-thirds society' became widespread. The conclusion of the New Left was that the aspirations embodied in the notion of the welfare state could only reach fruition through a more radical (socialist) transformation of society.

Meanwhile, the target of the New Right was bureaucracy, with its lack of accountability and its focus on serving its own ends. After their own fashion, critics of the welfare state among the New Right also called attention to the misuse of welfare benefits. In their view – following the reasoning of Friedrich Hayek – the ever-increasing tendency towards state intervention was equivalent to the road to serfdom, and in practice to the emergence of fascism, in which agreements among powerful interest groups prevail over the freedom-seeking individual. Weightier arguments were nevertheless deployed in the New Right's economic criticism, which noted that state meddling and the empowerment of bureaucracy reinforces inflationary tendencies, and that striving to maintain prosperity at all costs rigidifies the structure of the economy, ultimately hampering economic renewal and the rationalization of obsolete sectors. The mixed economy built on Keynesian foundations was contrasted with the flexibility of private enterprise, always striving for the optimum solution. However, it would take a crisis of welfare capitalism to occur before this criticism could coalesce into a practical manifesto.

Although the various theoretical criticisms would not in themselves have led to the dissolution of the welfare consensus, the ushering in of a new era in the global economy in the 1970s had an impact on the welfare systems of developed countries. The collapse of the international monetary system in 1971 and the explosion in oil prices after 1973 multiplied uncertainty factors in the global economy and undermined the reliability of economic planning. Changes in international economic conditions prompted structural and institutional adjustments in individual national economies. The slowdown in global economic growth starting in the early 1970s cast doubt on the generation of distributable surplus income. Welfare institutions were in many respects inextricable from the prosperity of the quarter-century in which they arose, and as this growth came to an end and stagflation kicked in, economic policy principles that had hitherto been seen as definitive – such as prioritizing employment and income policy – were called into question. Social issues slipped further down the political agenda, and governments locked horns increasingly often with trade unions, with a view to keeping the so-called wage–price spiral in check.

Withdrawal from the obligations of welfare provision was simplest and quickest in liberal systems, in which the welfare state was woven most loosely into the economic and social fabric. Within the space of a year in the United States, Ronald Reagan slashed various social programmes (home-building subsidies, schooling for children of low-income families, supplemental income for the physically disabled, etc.) to the tune of $10 billion, while increasing budgetary arms spending by a similar amount. It was Reagan who began to scale back progressivity in the tax system, with the expectation that a reduction in high tax rates would stimulate economic growth and with the promise that the fruits of this would then be consumed by the lower-earning layers of society ('trickle-down economics').

In the United Kingdom, Margaret Thatcher championed 'popular capitalism', but the social impact of her economic policies proved antithetical to neoconservative ideology. Under Thatcher, the proportion of families in which both adults worked grew, but at the same time so did the proportion of families containing no full-time workers: from 29% to 37%. All this only deepened inequalities. Excluding housing-related expenditures, the average British family's real income rose by 37% between 1979 and 1992. However, over the same period, real incomes decreased by 18% among the poorest tenth of society, while increasing by 61% among the richest tenth. In 1979 the richest tenth held some 20.6% of the nation's wealth, and the poorest tenth only 4.3%. Twelve years later, the respective figures stood at 26.1% and 2.9%.[11] As well as inequalities between social strata, Thatcherite policies deepened regional disparities in the United Kingdom.

From the sociological perspective, the most conspicuous product of Thatcherism was the appearance of millions of long-term unemployed and what has been termed the British 'underclass'. Thatcher

---

11   See Evans (1997, 117–118).

and the (active and passive) proponents of her policies were able to present a society split between the two-thirds living in prosperity and the one-third left behind as a natural phenomenon, and to shift responsibility for personal crises arising from unemployment and impaired material conditions onto the individuals concerned.[12] Armstrong (2018) demonstrates that the neoconservative reforms of the 1980s and the lack of forceful corrective interventions subsequently brought back into British society some of the problems Beveridge analysed and wanted to find a solution for.

In the English-speaking world from the late 1970s onwards, the responses of the New Right and neoconservatives to global crises represented a robust attack on state economic management and welfare redistribution, in theory and practice alike. The three-word formula of the new political right was 'liberalization, deregulation and privatization', as withdrawal from the social responsibilities of the state placed the partial marketization of welfare institutions on the agenda. New Right governments applied financial pressure to local governments and simultaneously launched political assaults against the trade unions safeguarding the achievements of social policy, significantly restricting unions' operations.

Despite the neoconservative hegemony and the appearance of new narratives, the welfare state did not perish; instead we can speak of a period of adaptation and innovation. The statistics do not necessarily reveal a reduction in welfare expenditure under neoconservative governments – not least because provision for unemployment demanded far greater sums than before due to the swelling ranks of the jobless. However, conditionality with respect to social support emerged in many places, so that receipt of unemployment benefits, for example, was increasingly tied to proof of seeking work or participation in training. Such conditional transfers were introduced earliest in less developed countries; their spread in developed economies,

---

12   The most striking example of this shifting of responsibility was an aphorism of then Secretary of State for Employment Norman Tebbit ('get on your bike'), in reference to Tebbit's father who, unemployed during the Great Depression, got on his bike to search for work, and found it. The solution to unemployment, from his point of view, was therefore a matter of individual aptitude, and not dependent on the ministrations or intervention of the state.

meanwhile, is explained by the desire for the welfare system not to replace but rather to complement high levels of employment and the resulting incomes.

STRIVING FOR A EUROPEAN SOCIAL MODEL

For a long time, the neoconservative wave being ridden in tandem by the British and the Americans appeared irresistible. Many already regarded the welfare state founded on a mixed economy more as a historical detour than as a golden age. Even so, neoconservatism was by no means the automatic direction to follow, and not every-one wished to conform to it, especially in Western Europe. For this reason, in the latter half of the 1980s the neoconservative United Kingdom came into conflict with the European Economic Com-munity (EEC), whose leaders had, in 1986, envisioned a strong social dimension as one of the objectives of the establishment of the single market.

The EEC, though primarily launched with the aim of economic integration, embraced social issues among its goals and instruments from the outset. The European Social Fund, assisting investment in human capital, was set up at the very beginning, in 1958. When the members of the EEC resolved to transform into a Union in the 1980s, the deepening of the social dimension became part of the core mission. Besides European nation states, the institutions of the EU emerged as regulators of working conditions, as well as assuming roles in shaping, coordinating and partly financing social policy.

At the time of the EU's formation, as it transformed from a Com-munity to a Union, the political leaders of most member countries were fully awake to the importance of the social dimension. This was particularly true of Jacques Delors, who presided over the European Commission for ten years between 1985 and 1995. Delors notably provoked the ire of Margaret Thatcher when he participated in the annual conference of trade unions in Brighton in 1988, where he promised the unions a major role in the governance of the single market. It was Delors who introduced the concept of the European social model into Brussels usage, elevating the tripartite conciliation of interests (also referred to as social dialogue) to the Union level in institutional form, and who pushed through the Community Charter of the Fundamental Social Rights of Workers in 1989. He launched labour legislation at the EU level and strengthened financial instruments in the EU budget that served social and regional cohesion.

Although it would have been impossible to establish the EU without defining the social dimension of integration, the actual construction of this social dimension took place only gradually, step by step, due to the related political controversies. EU laws were created for such issues as working hours, the rights of workers to information and consultation, equality in employment between men and women, the freedom to work in other countries of the Union, and health and accident protections in the workplace. Indeed, the EU's social policy – as defined in the Maastricht Treaty – essentially deals with labour issues and touches only indirectly and to a modest extent on the welfare systems of member countries. In its broadly defined social policy, the EU performs a supportive function while respecting the principle of subsidiarity.

At the same time, the social market economy as described in EU treaties also means that the social consequences of economic integration and competition among countries cannot be left to chance. Although the EU did not create the welfare systems of its member states, it is reasonable to expect that it will not endanger them. Indeed, wherever possible, economic integration should help fortify the social models of member states. To this end, the EU has three tools at its disposal: legislation, professional political coordination and budgetary instruments (albeit none of these are without their limits). Each of these has been part of the operations of the Union from the outset, essentially serving to maintain equilibrium in the single market.

In principle, therefore, since systems of welfare provision are not managed by the Union and welfare expenditures mostly constitute part of the budgets of member countries, the EU cannot assume ultimate responsibility with regard to social problems such as child poverty or homelessness. At the same time, for the sake of its credibility, the EU cannot remain indifferent to the social problems of member countries, regions and communities, but should use its own means to help alleviate them. It must take such problems into consideration when exercising its other (e.g. macroeconomic or market regulating) powers, when apportioning its own funds, when developing its external economic relationships, and above all when gauging the fulfilment of cohesion and convergence within the Union.

For the school of thought (and policy) established by Delors, the concept of 'social Europe' developed as an antithesis to a raw free-market Europe, opposing a model that would pay attention only to the economic gains of market integration and not to its distributional effects and other social consequences. Without questioning the primacy of national and subnational competencies in this field, expressing a commitment to social Europe represents an assurance that the EU does not seek to damage important aspects of social protection and national welfare models. To the contrary, the Union identifies with the missions and objectives of social policy within its member states, and through the integration it promotes and the coordination it performs it aims at further improving social outcomes.

Beyond cohesion and convergence, EU documents have increasingly often begun to use key notions such as 'well-being'. In this spirit, familiar measures of material prosperity (such as income levels, employment and poverty) have been joined by indicators such as mental health and environmental quality.[13] Even though unemployment around the turn of the millennium was much higher than it was during the 'golden age', it became increasingly important for governments to aim not only at expanding the number of workplaces, but also at improving job quality.

The enlargement of the EU in 1995, with the accession of three European Free Trade Association (EFTA) countries (Austria, Finland and Sweden), expanded the membership to include societies with strong social democratic traditions. At the same time, this enlargement served to widen the circle of members who regarded the safeguarding and consolidation of social achievements as primarily the province of the individual member states, not the Union as a

---

13   To map out indicators beyond GDP, French President Nicolas Sarkozy convened a commission in 2008 that was headed by Jean-Paul Fitoussi, Joseph Stiglitz and Amartya Sen. Work was coordinated on the part of the OECD by Enrico Giovannini, helping to make social progress measurable and laying the foundations for the economics of sustainability.

whole. Moreover, not even Scandinavia could escape international trends, as debate intensified over the sustainability of the Swedish model. As Northern Europe went through a financial crisis in the early 1990s, the search for an exit increasingly pointed towards more markets and less bureaucracy – and lower taxes. After the financial systems of Finland and Sweden collapsed, accession to the EU became an integral part of economic crisis management programmes, while conservatives argued that welfare redistribution and social rights – judged excessive by German or French standards – needed to be scaled back.

Embracing individual countries within a common economic framework based on the Maastricht Treaty, EU integration also targeted the introduction of a single currency, for which the fiscal and monetary indicators of the countries concerned needed to converge (or, more precisely, to approach the price stability performance of exemplar countries). The world of work and welfare systems remained, comparatively, a secondary issue from the perspective of integration. Nevertheless, important initiatives were built on the foundations laid by Delors, including the Lisbon Strategy,[14] adopted in 2000, and – once the latter had run its course – the Europe 2020 Strategy, adopted in 2010. The European social model remained a point of reference throughout, demonstrating a continuing commitment to advanced labour relations, high levels of employment and social protections.

EUROPEAN COMPLICATIONS: FOUR CHALLENGES

Despite the continuous expansion of social (or, more accurately, labour) legislation and the introduction of successive coordination and financing mechanisms, actors and experts invested in a social

---

14   Heads of state and government at the Lisbon Summit (March 2000) set the EU the goal of making the Union 'the most competitive and dynamic knowledge-based economy in the world, capable of sustainable economic growth with more and better jobs and greater social cohesion'. The initiative reflected the intellectual leadership of Portuguese economist Maria João Rodrigues. With respect to the social dimension, the so-called open method of coordination (OMC) was introduced for implementation of the Lisbon Strategy.

Europe characterize the past quarter-century more as a series of set-backs, regressions and erosions than as a straight line of development. If the debates of the 1990s revolved around the end of the welfare state, the same is even truer of Western European discourse today. Moreover, most European countries after 2008 endured unprecedented economic shocks, which triggered social consequences that were difficult to manage.

The experiences of the past two decades have shaken the belief that the EU helped to consolidate the system of welfare capitalism that had evolved earlier. Four major transformations have played key roles in this, representing what are commonly seen as deadly threats to the European social model. These four horsemen of the apocalypse are none other than globalization, European monetary union, the eastward expansion of the EU, and the digital and automation revolution.

I understand globalization to mean intensifying international transactions and the deepening of primarily financial and trade connections, as well as the process of bringing down barriers to those connections around the globe. Thanks to evolving technology and the falling costs of transport and communication, new frontiers have opened up for the countries of the world, with administrative barriers dismantled by states themselves in the hope of mutually beneficial transactions. More intensive investment and trade relations have stimulated a greater volume of migration, and liberalization has unshackled the movement of international capital. The latter change has provided a new impetus to the building of multinational corporate empires, leading to the creation of power centres in global private enterprise that are increasingly able to influence the politics of states in which they operate, upsetting the hitherto-prevalent balance of power within individual states. At the same time, by accelerating the internationalization of production and capital, the neoconservative offensive has substantially weakened the institutions of the nation state that provide the framework for macroeconomic management and welfare systems in a national context. Increasingly intense economic competition on a global scale for the more advanced countries has started to erode the material foundations of the welfare state (Glyn 2006), making it harder to sustain full employment, or even merely a commitment to ensuring some level of job security.

The second challenge to the European social model – and one that poses problems for the social dimension of the EU as a whole in addition to the welfare state in a national context – is the currency union. A monetary union established without unified financial supervision and common fiscal capacity is similar, in an economic sense, to the operation of a currency board, in that it shifts economic policy towards pan-European monetarism. In essence this means that, without a flexible national currency, internal devaluation becomes almost inevitable in any crisis situation; in other words, countries of the periphery will try to restore their fiscal balance and enhance their competitiveness at the expense of their welfare systems and often by surrendering some of the more central features of their social models. Although negative effects had already appeared before the introduction of the single currency (in the period of compliance with the newly introduced Maastricht criteria in the 1990s), aspects of social cohesion have been increasingly subordinated to the maintenance of short-term fiscal equilibrium since the establishment of Economic and Monetary Union (EMU), and in particular since the EMU crisis. Convergence within the EU has ceased, with the community splitting into two groups of countries: in one, thanks to a higher level of fiscal and financial stability, the welfare state survives and continues to develop; in the other, by contrast, the functioning of the labour market and the welfare system depends on the fluctuations of boom and bust. This process cannot be counterbalanced by means of social policy alone: what is needed is a comprehensive rethink of the structure and operation of the monetary union.

The third trend – once celebrated but now frequently criticized – is the eastward expansion of the EU. The integration of countries with considerably lower levels of productivity and income into the EU's single market during its enlargement eastward created the opportunity for 'social dumping' within the Union. What is more, the (comparatively) new Eastern European member countries harbour a significantly greater number of politicians who are not committed to the European social model, and who moreover subscribe to the idea that a lower standard of social provision is one possible means of enhancing economic competitiveness. One consequence of the east–west gulf in productivity and wages is that capital largely flows from west to east, and jobs mainly from east to west. In Western European (and Northern European) countries with advanced welfare systems and higher average wages, newly arriving workers from Eastern Europe appear as a threat in terms of both competition for jobs and the uptake of socially provisioned services. Fears of social dumping and of the social consequences of eastward expansion in general have sparked endless debate (e.g. with respect to so-called posted workers), and they also contributed in a significant way to the outcome of the 2016 British referendum on EU membership.

The fourth main trend is the technological revolution (the rise of robots and digitalization), which provokes euphoria or panic in turn among economic and social actors. In the case of globalization and the close integration of advanced and poorer economies, it is the migration of jobs and the appearance of cheap foreign labour that threatens the security of employment on the side of the more advanced economies. In this case, it is the abrupt evolution of technology that triggers similar fears. If robots take over various tasks en masse, then job and income security will disappear for a large number of today's workers. Simultaneous innovations in work processes and the welfare system might prove the answer to this challenge. Those urging the introduction of an unconditional basic income (UBI), for example, see the robot revolution – by supplanting living labour – as depriving a great many workers of a stable income, pushing UBI's rapid launch onto the agenda. Following the success of futuristic writings on digitalization and automation, analyses by the OECD and the International Labour Organization have shifted the debate in a more realistic direction, demonstrating that, at least in the foreseeable future, the digital revolution will have a greater impact on the quality of jobs than on their quantity. Predictions concerning the digital revolution and its consequences for labour are at times exaggerated: consequences that may eventuate fifty to sixty years from now do not necessarily imply a collapse in the short term. What remains beyond doubt, however, is that trends in digitalization and automation both in the economy and in everyday life are unfolding very rapidly indeed, changing the quality of work and life and transforming social conditions.

The four transformations listed above genuinely challenge – and are consequently reshaping – the welfare systems that had evolved earlier. That being said, this does not mean that they must inevitably be perceived as an existential blow or unqualified source of danger. Besides risks they also bring opportunities, as enforced transformation and adaptation also carry the incentive to innovate and achieve greater performance.

In the next portion of the book I will devote a chapter each to examining the four trends threatening European welfare states. We will see that, with appropriate technological, organizational and financial innovations, as well as institutional reforms, the negative impacts of the four major trends can be mitigated and their positive effects amplified. At the same time, the concurrence of the four trends makes implementation of such innovations considerably more difficult, which in turn may have repercussions on expectations and political aspirations regarding both the future of the welfare state and the fate of European integration.

Following analysis of the four trends, I will review how the EU strove to reconstitute its own social dimension in the wake of the Great Recession of 2009 and the eurozone crisis. Finally, I will assess the impact of the Covid-19 crisis, which in essence pertains to strengthening and deepening social and healthcare cooperation within the framework of the EU, thus defying stereotypes that can be found not only in the world of politics but also in social science.

Global competition and social divides

GLOBALISM AND NEOLIBERALISM

To say that globalism and neoliberalism – as two intertwined trends – have reshaped the global economy, widening social divides and endangering the welfare systems of developed countries, is to speak primarily of the processes of the last quarter of the twentieth century. We need only look back to the global economic crisis of the 1970s to find the turning point in economic policy and broader political thinking that led to an overall change of direction in world politics.

As far as economic policy is concerned, the stagflation of the 1970s took the wind out of the sails of Keynes-inspired, reform-oriented liberalism. The economists who dictated the new vogue placed the blame for the crisis on state intervention, and particularly on policies aimed at full employment and significant taxation of high incomes. Milton Friedman, the father of the monetarist school of economics, proclaimed that the task of the state is not to eliminate unemployment but rather to allow it to evolve at its 'natural rate'. Arthur Laffer endeavoured to prove that 'overtaxation' of the economy holds back economic activity; accordingly, he argued, tax rates should be reduced by all means possible, not least because the expected revival of the economy could even ultimately result in an increase in tax revenues. The elderly Friedrich Hayek stubbornly held to the belief that all kinds of state intervention lead society down the road to serfdom, and that even money itself should be denationalized.

It would require a set of separate studies to investigate the validity of these theories that championed a return to free-market solutions, often cited together under the umbrella term 'neoliberal'. Nevertheless, the fact remains that it was while proclaiming slogans derived from these theories that the governments of the 1980s (above all, those of Margaret Thatcher and Ronald Reagan) opposed any and all factors that limited the room for manoeuvre of capital and businesses, including trade unions, state redistribution and aid for developing countries.

Neoliberalism is partly a continuation, but in certain respects also the antithesis, of earlier versions of liberalism. Originally, liberalism signified progress, proclaiming modernization and social advancement.

However, neoliberal thinking in economics was able to prevail largely under right-wing, neoconservative political leaders, who discarded the classical notion of a balance between the ideals of freedom and equality. The English liberalism of the nineteenth century primarily brought its influence to bear on the continent and the wider world not through its doctrines but rather through its concrete technical and economic achievements, chiefly in the wake of the Great Exhibition of 1851. The situation was similar with the liberalism that was reborn in the spirit of the New Deal as part of the growth trajectory of the 'golden age' of the 1950s and 1960s. By contrast, late-twentieth-century neoliberalism focused not on performance but on the choice of method: a state-owned production plant or service does not become unfit for purpose because it is unprofitable, but simply because it is not under private ownership; a trade policy intervention is not to be curtailed because it might be dysfunctional, but simply because it exists.

Under the most commonly held interpretation, globalization and neoliberalism are closely intertwined processes. One important element of the neoliberal breakthrough was financial and trade liberalization, which provided impetus to the expansion of transnational companies. After a while, certain multilateral organizations became the driving force of the neoliberal trend across the globe. The Washington-based financial organizations – the International Monetary Fund and the World Bank – transplanted the neoliberal philosophy into the developing and emerging economies on the periphery of the global system. The outbreak of the global debt crisis played its role in the ability of the two Washington institutions to achieve this, since it enabled the IMF to attach strict conditions to standby loans. These conditions – which went beyond a narrowly conceived macroeconomic framework – had to be fulfilled by governments within a short time frame. The World Bank's programme loans played a similar role, with the difference being that these so-called structural adjustment loans set the duration of the transformation to a longer period (of generally three, and sometimes four, years). Although indebted countries typically did not fulfil every condition, the two institutions were still able to mark out the main direction of institutional development in the global south, where, not long before, emerging countries had urged the rest of the world to accept the manifesto of the New International Economic Order under the aegis of the United Nations.

The concept of globalization,[1] which has been a key concept in social science over the past thirty to forty years, essentially covers the period of the neoliberal paradigm shift, without being understood in the same way by all those who use the term. Depending on the prevailing wave of intellectual fashion, it appears in the public discourse sometimes as the root of all evil and sometimes – in the absence of an alternative – as the inevitable fulfilment of global historical progress. Irrespective of any value judgement attached to the term, the period and process to which 'globalization' most often refers (principally in the economic literature) began in the 1970s, with the emergence of transnational corporations and international financial liberalization. One phenomenon that accompanied the process was the debt crisis in the developing world, which brought numerous countries in Latin America, Africa and East Asia to their knees both economically and socially, and during which Pinochet-era Chile served as a laboratory for economic policy. This type of globalism was closely intertwined not only with the concept of neoliberalism but also with Americanization, not least because after 1989 the so-called Washington Consensus encapsulated the economic policy prescriptions of globalization.

The Washington Consensus was the name given to a set of prescriptions for stripping back the functions of the state, and in

---

1   Especially important in the Hungarian literature on globalization are Ágh (1987) and Csáki and Farkas (2008).

the 1990s it was proclaimed as a universal recipe for government.[2] According to the neoliberal interpretation of globalization, the new global situation permitted no (civilized) alternative to this trend. The somewhat two-dimensional recipe of the Washington Consensus thus implied integration into the international financial system and fulfilment of the conditions for financial reliability. It was a set of principles designed to ensure the efficient utilization of the funds that were provided by international financial organizations and capital markets: in this way, a particular country's economy could be made ready to both receive external funding and pay back loans.

The Washington economic policy – essentially summarizing the consensus that had evolved between the IMF and the World Bank by the end of the 1980s – is primarily described as neoliberal not by its proponents but by its critics. Proponents of the doctrine see themselves as liberal, libertarian or conservative, depending on cultural and political parameters. The epithet neoliberal is used (with a critical edge) primarily by those who regard the motivating ideals of the proponents of the Washington Consensus – such as the attraction to romanticized laissez-faire ideas, the preference for small government at the expense of all else, and above all the attempt at the end of the twentieth century to restore classical liberal economic institutions – as an anachronistic return to the principles of nineteenth-century 'Manchester' liberalism and a grave aberration and misstep in economic and social history.

Besides the Washington Consensus proclaiming the 'end of history' in the economic sense, the other main reason we may regard the 1990s as the heyday of (neoliberal) globalism is the formation of the

---

2   The expression 'Washington Consensus' was coined by John Williamson at a conference organized by the Institute for International Economics in 1990. The prescriptions of the Washington Consensus can be summarized as follows: (1) fiscal discipline; (2) changed priorities in public spending; (3) broadening the tax base; (4) financial liberalization; (5) safe, export-stimulating exchange rate policy; (6) liberalization of foreign trade (which, together with point 5, signifies liberalization of current account transactions); (7) liberalization of inward foreign direct investment (in practice, liberalization of capital operations); (8) privatization; (9) full deregulation; and (10) security of property rights.

World Trade Organization (WTO) in 1995. With this, the international community (but primarily the OECD countries) bypassed the incremental dismantling of obstacles to trade by attempting to set down general and universal rules for the free movement of goods. In a certain sense, this represented a return to the spirit of negotiation that followed World War II. At that time, however, free trade would not have gone hand in hand with the entirely free movement of capital, which by the end of the century had become almost a fundamental principle. The creation of the WTO would essentially spell the end of convergence efforts built on protectionism (development via import substitution), while the endeavour to bring Russia and China into the WTO fold demonstrated the demand for universality.

GLOBALIZED COMPETITION AND WELFARE RETRENCHMENT

The neoliberal trend that was spearheaded by multilateral institutions would facilitate the consummation of globalism by the 1990s, after the Soviet Union and its international network of allies disintegrated and the bloc of countries that had previously functioned as a community of planned economies also chose integration into the free-trading world economic order. The fallout from global economic crises, combined with neoconservative assaults, drove state-socialist systems into a crisis of their own that eventually led to their collapse at the end of the 1980s, shaking the ideological and social foundations of Western reformist aspirations. After all, if no one continued to defend the idea of central planning, then the attraction of a hybrid approach, somewhere between a planned and a market economy, would only be weakened further. In this way, globalism put pressure on the welfare models of developed countries not only directly (via financial, trade and economic policy channels) but also ideologically.

The end of the Cold War – especially in countries that had invested heavily in arms and their armed forces – held out the promise of a peace dividend, albeit not for very long. The new globalized environment was detrimental from the point of view of wage dynamics, as demonstrated by the stagnation that took hold over several decades in the United States. At times of economic crisis, public welfare expenditures were fixed in the crosshairs, as economic policymakers sought potential ways to whittle them down. Competitiveness became an increasingly important consideration, as national governments took the side of capital by attempting to strengthen companies' international competitiveness through helping to shave wages and wage-related costs. The reduction in taxes – and their burden on profits, high personal incomes and enterprises – resulted in increased inequalities and, if those taxes were not replaced by other revenues, also narrowed the options for welfare redistribution.

Simultaneously to these processes of economic restructuring, the steady ageing of societies in advanced capitalist countries was becoming an increasingly evident trend, placing ever-growing demand on ever-dwindling financial resources. In the United States, for example, while there was one dependent pensioner for every nine active earners at the end of the 1930s, by the 1990s this had risen to one for every three. Due to commitments undertaken in earlier decades, the growing proportion of the elderly in the population exerts constant pressure on healthcare expenditures and pensions. The welfare state is caught in a pincer movement between pressurized public revenues and growing needs.

For all these economic, political and demographic reasons, from the early 1990s the view took hold – and no longer only in the English-speaking countries – that welfare provision had reached its reasonable limits, and indeed even needed to be scaled back. A growing number of analysts began to speak in the past tense about the welfare states that evolved after World War II, or at least interpreted developments in the 1980s as the beginning of a new era in terms of possible paths for the future. Although approaches, theoretical backgrounds and proposals for alternatives may have differed, the emphasis was typically on discontinuity. A new narrative emerged around the decline of the welfare state – a decline that Pierson (1991) directly attributed to its incompatibility with a 'healthy' market economy in the long term. It was only after the war, in conditions that were exceptionally favourable from the perspective of economic growth, that the economy and the welfare state were able to flourish simultaneously. Under the conditions of globalized competition, economic growth cannot be rebooted without drastically pruning back social redistribution.

Even if the emergence of the welfare state was an organic part of the development of modern capitalist societies, as many have taken it to be, its period of extraordinary growth remains historically anomalous. The welfare state has reached its 'growth limits', and each newly proposed element can now be expected to encounter resistance. The welfare consensus has either broken down or only continued to protect a narrowing circle of individual national models. The post-war welfare state represented a historical compromise between the powers and interests of capital and organized labour. However, while welfare state policies once served the interests of both parties, they have since become less and less attractive to either and are now able to mobilize only ever-dwindling support among the two camps.

The strength of the conservative hegemony is demonstrated by the fact that many regard not merely the welfare state itself but Keynesian economic policy as a whole to be irreconcilable with the new model of the global economy. Accordingly, changes in the global economic order have made it increasingly difficult to sustain national welfare states. In a certain sense, the expansion of welfare benefits (particularly in the areas of public health and education) has itself brought about social changes, calling into question the further need for social transfers. Most importantly, however, the evolution of the welfare state has transformed the class structure in developed capitalist societies, thereby slowly undermining the class basis for its own survival. These changes have shaken the alliance of the middle and working classes on which the welfare state was built, encouraging a growing proportion of the population to turn their backs on public welfare benefits and withdraw their support for them. The expansion of consumer choice and affluence in western industrialized economies has led to growing dissatisfaction with state-administered welfare, with the result that consumers increasingly turn to welfare services available on the open market.

While this growing hesitation over the welfare state does not necessarily mean its achievements are questioned, it has led to the loss of prospects for further development. Some have taken the view that, while the welfare state can be seen as historically progressive, further progress is not viable without a substantial transformation of welfare policies. This is because the welfare state is tied to a productivist economic growth strategy, the environmental impact of which means it is no longer reconcilable with the fulfilment of actual human needs and with guarantees of genuine social well-being.

The above reflections approached the question of the sustainability of the welfare state in an eclectic manner, drawing on a variety of paradigms. Beyond narrowly defined social policy, they revealed a far more diverse phenomenon, pointing to a complex set of problems encompassing politics, economics, social psychology and more. And yet, despite their diversity, these theses convincingly demonstrate that the consensus that prevailed until the end of the 1970s, which regarded the welfare state as the 'end of history', had been replaced by the end of the 1980s and beginning of the 1990s by a new consensus that instead signalled the end of the welfare state – at least in the form it had taken until then. In post-war Western Europe, the welfare state appeared to be an integrative project that united the various layers of society. It was the neoliberal paradigm shift that began to separate the minority dependent on the welfare state (i.e. benefits) from the majority of society, thus transforming it into an instrument of division.

The OECD attempted to interpret the situation and find a way forward with its Jobs Strategy published in 1994, which reflected the neoliberal spirit of the age (Mahon 2011). It did so by pushing for reforms of job security, or – in clearer terms – by urging flexibility in the labour market and the wider application of fixed-term employment, while also calling for incentives to be incorporated into the system of unemployment benefits in order to encourage people to actively attempt to return to work. The paradigm represented by the OECD did not fail to have an impact on the EU's first Employment Strategy (1997) or on the labour market policies of individual EU member states.

One classic example of labour market reform comes from Germany. In contrast to neoconservative Britain, in West Germany no significant qualitative change in the labour market or the system of social benefits occurred until the end of the 1980s – something that can largely be attributed to the latter country's superior economic performance and its commitment to the social market model (tripartism in particular). At the same time, high unemployment kept wage dynamics in check in Germany, especially after unification, when an unemployment rate close to 10% became a constant feature.[3] Under Chancellor Gerhard Schröder, comprehensive labour reforms were implemented with the cooperation of an expert named Peter Hartz (then Volkswagen's HR director). The option of early retirement was rolled back, while earnings-related unemployment benefits were limited to one year (with the option of fixed social benefits beyond that term). A kind of mythology evolved around the Hartz reforms (Odendahl 2017), which became a frequent base of reference in other countries, where attempts were made – because of, or even in the absence of, high unemployment – to increase employment levels and strengthen economic competitiveness by reworking labour market regulations and the system of social support.

WIDENING INCOME GAPS

The social impact of the neoliberal era can best be measured by the way in which inequalities have multiplied. This is not merely a matter of the income deciles at opposite poles moving further apart; instead, it has involved the complete breakaway of the richest 1% of earners. In recent years, attention has been brought to bear on the privileged status of this group through social movements such as Occupy in the United States, who protested by taking over public spaces and buildings. According to OECD data, in thirty-four member countries (essentially the most developed nations) in the 1970s, the incomes of the richest 10% of earners were seven times greater than those of the poorest 10%. By the turn of the millennium, this discrepancy had grown to ten times greater – even in comparatively egalitarian countries such as Norway and Sweden. In the so-called emerging countries, the gap was far more conspicuous: the incomes of the richest 10% were 30 times greater than those of the poorest 10% in Mexico, 50 times greater in Brazil and 100 times greater in South Africa.

---

3   The German unemployment rate exceeded 10% only in the 2004–6 period.

The French economist Thomas Piketty[4] has produced data identifying the mid 1970s as the turning point that opened the way towards a weakening – and in some places, dismantlement – of the welfare states that had been built up after World War II. Progressive taxation was pruned back, as was public ownership and the influence of the trade unions. This mainstream trend, for which Reagan and Thatcher are the classic political figureheads, was not confined to right-wing political forces. Social democrats of the so-called Third Way also reconciled themselves to the growing inequalities: as the former British minister Peter Mandelson once put it, they were 'intensely relaxed about people getting filthy rich'. But the heyday of Clintonism and Blairism is now distant history, and no responsible political school of thought can remain indifferent to this problem of inequality.

Within what is regarded as the developed world, the United States shows the greatest degree of inequality by far; even twenty-five years ago, incomes in the uppermost decile were already ten times greater than in the lowest decile, and by now they are sixteen-and-a-half times greater. Moreover, if we look at the very top 1% within the uppermost decile, we see that this tiny group pockets as much as 8% of all untaxed income. Even in Canada, this same uppermost one-thousandth of the population earns 'only' 4% of the total. Although Piketty reviews trends over several hundreds of years, he leaves no doubt that the end of the 1970s represented an unprecedented turning point. During the Keynesian era in the United States (1948–78), the wealth possessed by the top 1% fell from 30% to 23% of the country's total; then, over the following thirty-five years of the neoliberal period (1978–2012), it swelled from 23% to 42%.

---

4   In 2014 Thomas Piketty published his magnum opus *Capital in the Twenty-First Century*, which quickly became a bestseller and was translated into numerous languages. A thinker of the political left, Piketty was born into the generation that grew up following the Cold War. His work analysing capitalism, though critical of inequalities, does not mean that he feels any sympathy towards the Soviet-type systems that existed before 1989. He believes that it is easier for his generation to reopen the debate on inequality – and that they must do so before it is too late.

Since the start of the era of globalization, average real wages in the most developed countries have either stagnated (as in the United States) or only barely risen (as in Western Europe), while income disparities have soared. Real wages and salaries have not grown since the early 1970s in the United States, since the early 1980s in Europe and since the late 1980s in Japan, with the wage share in production steadily shrinking as a consequence. Wage differentiation has accelerated particularly sharply in the United States (before we even begin to talk about the ratio of capital income to wages). While in many cases the pay of managers and senior executives has skyrocketed, the purchasing power of unskilled or low-skilled workers has stagnated in Europe and decreased in the United States. For example, average annual wages for American men fell from $34,000 in 1973 to $30,000 in 1993 (reckoning with the value of the US dollar in 1993), while real GDP per capita increased by 29%. Only the uppermost 20% of workers were able to enjoy wage increases (of 10%) over the twenty years in question, while the other four-fifths of the working population suffered drops in the value of their annual pay ranging from 10% to 23%, with the bottom fifth enduring the greatest decline.

Piketty and other economists such as Joseph Stiglitz and Tony Atkinson[5] have demonstrated not only that inequalities have intensified but also that they are economically harmful. Those at the peak of the income scale do not contribute anywhere near as much to the expansion of national economies as the amount by which they have enriched themselves since the 1970s. To put it another way, just as the fight against poverty is in the public interest, so too is taxation of the highest incomes and assets, and the prevention of their further growth. In his books and interviews, Piketty points out how wars have often led to progressive change – such as in France, where personal income tax was introduced at the outbreak of World War I to help finance the war effort. At the same time, he believes

---

5   Other important authors on the topic of inequality include Angus Deaton (winner of the Nobel Prize in 2015) and the British geographer Danny Dorling (with his book on the top 1%), as well as Wilkinson and Pickett (2009) and Therborn (2013), who have exposed the impact of income inequalities on health and demographics.

change can also be achieved peacefully by relying on progressive social movements. It sounds utopian, but Piketty bluntly proposes a global wealth tax to reverse the growing trend of inequality. Today, even the OECD speaks in similarly blunt terms when it notes that, where inequalities decrease, economic performance improves, and where they increase, performance declines.

The financial and economic crisis of 2008–9 (which ended sooner in America than in Europe) took a heavy toll on societies every-where, and with few exceptions it led to a further increase in income and wealth inequalities. Those who lost their jobs or homes, or part of their working incomes or pensions, suffered the most. Though the crisis presented an opportunity to correct the previous model of economic development, in most places this opportunity was not exploited; in other words, neoliberalism as a doctrine, though shaken, was far from extinguished. The old model soon returned: wealth still accumulates at the top of the income scale, while the belt-tightening continues at the bottom and the middle class continues to shrink.

At the same time, in the years following the Great Recession, major international institutions such as the OECD and the IMF also began to speak in anxious tones about inequalities. It is to this inquiring audience, searching for an alternative, that Piketty con-veys his weighty message; namely, that growing inequality derives from the very functioning of capital and is an essential part of the capitalist system itself. Though it can be corrected, it requires serious efforts and institutional transformation – the like of which was only seen in the OECD countries during the quarter-century following World War II.

An examination of the income dynamics of the neoliberal era is revealing not only when focusing on individual countries but also when taking a global economic perspective. A summary of the income processes attributed to globalization is provided in the work of Branko Milanović (2005, 2010), in which he uses the so-called elephant curve to demonstrate that it is the middle class and skilled workers in developed countries who have suffered most in the past twenty-five years, while the super-rich in OECD countries and society more broadly in emerging economies (primarily thanks to China) have been able to record the most rapid gains.

Looking at the last two decades of the twentieth century, we can see that, in the most developed countries, per capita income grew from an annual $18,000 in 1980 to $26,000 by the end of the millennium (measured in GDP, and using the value of the US dollar and exchange rates in 1993). In the rapidly industrializing Far East – minus China – it grew from $1,200 to $2,500, and in China from $200 to $800. Over this same two-decade period, it rose from $200 to $350 in South Asia, but only marginally in Latin America, from $3,300 to $3,400; meanwhile, it declined from $6,200 to $3,500 in Western Asia, from $800 to $650 in Africa, from $300 to $250 in the group of least developed countries, and from $2,200 to $1,200 in Eastern Europe. Of the world population of 6 billion in the year 2000, close to 2 billion were living in regions and countries where, over the aforementioned two decades, per capita GDP grew by less than $100–$150 annually (around a third of a dollar per day), which – in combination with a less equal distribution of incomes within these societies – signifies no perceptible improvement in the living standards of the majority of the population. A further 1.5 billion people were living in zones and continents where per capita income had declined.

At the turn of the millennium, roughly four-fifths of the population of our planet were living in economically underdeveloped countries. At that time, these countries had a share of total global income (GDP) of approximately 20% at official conversion rates, or 37% when calculated using purchasing power parity. The income gap between the developed and the 'developing' world has been growing at an accelerating pace. In terms of per capita income, the difference was twofold to three-fold in the mid nineteenth century, growing to ninefold by the mid twentieth century, and at the turn of this millennium it had already grown to twentyfold to twenty-six-fold (calculating with an average of $26,000 in developed countries versus $1,280 in the underdeveloped world when including the 'little Asian tigers' – Hong Kong, Singapore, South Korea and Taiwan – and $1,000 without them). Using the above measures, it can also clearly be seen that the gaps have expanded rapidly within the group of developing economies. Dividing 108 developing countries into fifths based on average income, the number of countries falling into the lowest fifth grew from 50 to 84 between 1965 and 1996. The late-twentieth-century wave of neoliberal and transnational globalization has thus left intensifying differentiating tendencies in its wake, both internationally and within individual societies, and in the central countries of the world order, its semi-periphery and its periphery alike.

EMERGING SAFETY NETS

The significance – or very existence – of neoliberal globalism has been cast into doubt, or been subject to attempts to relativize it, by those who hold that the world order has always displayed a tendency towards unification and integration, citing as an example the high degree of global integration brought about in the second half of the nineteenth century. There was indeed such a period, as is clear from the expansion of global trade in the half-century leading up to World War I, or even the course of migration (for which the primary target country at that time was the rapidly developing United States). Although we can therefore speak of successive waves of globalization, we cannot disregard the fact that the two waves in question represent globalization in two different forms, and that the lengthy intervening period was characterized by divergent models and by less open, more nationally focused development. After World War II and the interruption of globalized market conditions, it was this national framework that facilitated an economic golden age and the creation of the welfare state.

The growth of global inequalities after the 1970s – and above all the debt crises and the poverty that exploded in their wake – could not continue without a response. A section of world public opinion began looking for ways to offer assistance, whether ad hoc or more lasting solutions. Two manifestations of this sense of solidarity were the mobilization of pop musicians in the 1985 Live Aid concert, which urged a more efficient distribution of aid, and the activities of various solidarity networks. Movements were launched against commercial banks' exploitation of developing countries (e.g. the Lloyds and Midland Boycott, or LAMB), as was an international campaign for the cancellation of external debt.[6]

---

6   Jubilee 2000 lined up personalities such as the Irish rock singer Bono and the economists Jeffrey Sachs and Ann Pettifor.

More important than these ad hoc acts of solidarity, however, was the need for a change of direction in the institutions that were forcing through neoliberal policies and promoting the Washington Consensus. At the IMF, no substantive change occurred until the major crisis of 2008. Unlike the IMF, however, a certain degree of adjustment was perceptible at the World Bank after the Australian James Wolfensohn became president in 1995. His later senior vice president, Joseph Stiglitz, became one of the world's leading critics of the intransigent IMF – and of American neoconservatism. During Stiglitz's vice presidency, the World Bank's team of analysts opened up to the perspective of institutional economics, while Stiglitz himself initiated what came to be known as the post-Washington Consensus, moving away from the package of programmes elaborated ten years earlier. The Wolfensohn–Stiglitz experiment did not last long, however, after the younger President Bush installed one of the main architects of the Iraq War, Paul Wolfowitz, as president of the World Bank. Wolfowitz resolved to transform the institution into a spearhead in the global fight against corruption – which, in effect, translated to increased control over the functioning of national governments – and after his departure in 2007 the war on poverty once again became a target mission of the institution, in many respects revising earlier practice that had departed from programmes of enforced liberalization.

Signalling that global economic development required new institutional frameworks, the four strongest emerging economies – Brazil, Russia, India and China, commonly known by the acronym BRIC – formed a cooperative partnership. The four countries also established a joint development bank, which was joined after the Great Recession by the Asian Infrastructure Investment Bank (AIIB), launched in 2016 and with headquarters in Beijing.

More positive assessments of globalization hold that, despite initial problems, the process eventually bore fruit: after the turn of the millennium, global economic hierarchies loosened, developing countries truly developed and began to be called 'emerging' instead of 'developing', and a strong group of such emerging economies stood out in the shape of the BRIC countries. However, it is more appropriate and accurate to regard this as the second phase of globalization rather than as a direct consequence of the first (neoliberal) phase. The millennial convergence stories only came about by breaking away from the Washington Consensus, with even the Washington twins (the IMF and World Bank) endeavouring to reinvent themselves. In reality, therefore, what was now up for discussion was a correction or a new phase of globalization.

The three most significant emerging economies – China, India and Brazil – have become known in the past decade not only for having GDP growth more rapid than the average for the world economy, but also for their programmes to tackle poverty. China introduced a guaranteed minimum income model for its cities, under the name of the *dibao* programme. The party conference of November 2013 also launched reforms of the so-called *hukou* system, which were designed to bring the social rights of urban and rural populations closer together. Many observers have studied India's school meals scheme, as well as the rural employment guarantee model named after Mahatma Gandhi, which essentially extends the minimum wage to the informal economy: public services are obligated to offer work to those who apply for it, and whoever does not receive such an offer within a given deadline is entitled to benefits. Brazil's social programme – the Bolsa Família – has become a symbol of sorts. It is the first significant example of what are known as conditional cash transfers: in the case of the Bolsa Família, families receive a regular allowance in return for sending their children to school. Major sporting events over the past decade in Brazil were also tied to such schemes, which break up slum neighbourhoods in major cities and set the children of poor families on the path of education.

World Bank statistics show that the number of people covered by some form of social safety net (that is, benefiting from direct income transfers without the need to pay contributions) is increasing by 9% annually. Today a total of 1 billion people receive social transfers in some form. Around the turn of the millennium, the UN and the World Bank – and, after the major financial crisis, the G20 forum – each played a part in ensuring that social advances kept pace with economic development among the goals and activities of governments in Africa, South Asia and Latin America.

Besides these institutions and forums, the International Labour Organization (ILO) collaborates effectively in the improvement of labour laws and in creating decent conditions in the world of work. This process focuses on four key areas: minimum wages, maximum weekly working hours, maternity leave, and health and safety in the workplace. A minimum wage exists in 90% of ILO member countries – though in many cases it only applies to certain sectors. As far as working hours are concerned, only 8% of member countries have no specific, legally prescribed maximum number of weekly working hours. Cases such as the 2013 Rana Plaza factory tragedy in Bangladesh have prompted an accelerated reworking and modernization of labour laws. Naturally, pressure from trading partners (primarily the EU and the United States) has also played a role in speeding things up.

This evolution can have repercussions for more developed regions, and thus for Europe as well – even in light of the fact that regulatory or redistributive programmes in the developing world are often initially only about intentions and aspirations, and that it takes time for their effects to be palpably felt. The appearance of elements of the welfare state demonstrates that, although the social gulf between advanced and emerging economies may be wide, it can be narrowed; moreover, this convergence can be brought about not only through a weakening of the social systems in more developed countries, but also by strengthening the social dimension in emerging economies.

Based on a thorough study of this recent phase of correction, Phillips (2020) makes an important addition to the analysis of global inequalities. In keeping with Piketty, he presents the quarter-century following World War II as an exceptional period during which income inequalities were pushed back, but he also regards the first ten to twelve years of the new millennium as a similarly exceptional period for the countries of Latin America. Phillips sees this more recent period of development as having primarily been driven not by the aforementioned poverty-combating transfers but by changes that enabled wage increases, as well as by land reforms and the expansion of social services.

Europe's welfare models, despite their internal contradictions and struggles, thus serve as a pattern and inspiration for the rest of the world to follow. Countries in Asia and Latin America alike observe European examples; beyond a certain point, the economic convergence of emerging countries creates the need for social consolidation, with the establishment of more advanced social insurance and other social reforms. Of course, one could say that it is no surprise when richer countries strengthen their social safety nets – after all, 'they can afford it'. For this very reason, it is important to point out that the welfare state has found a foothold in other parts of the world economy, including in the so-called emerging regions. The past decade and a half can be interpreted as a kind of turning point in this regard.

We can also cite examples from more recent years of the ongoing evolution of welfare in OECD countries. These include the universal healthcare insurance introduced in the United States (Obamacare), as well as Germany's minimum wage. The former – though subject to fierce political attacks aimed at frustrating or destroying it – signals that even under the very liberal American model the time has come to open a new chapter in the development of welfare policy. After the Republican Party conquered the battleground states known for their declining industries, the Democrats needed to recognize that they would only have a chance of regaining power if they strengthened the European-style social democratic elements of their platform.

The need for democratization and the preservation of social and political stability is what helps a social state evolve, and this applies just as much outside the regions where the welfare state first appeared in the late nineteenth and early twentieth centuries. Measures guaranteeing social harmony can have a positive impact on willingness to invest, as well as on the cultivation of human resources. As the economies of emerging countries become more based on wage labour, so too will those countries strive to strengthen their social dimension. There is no irreconcilable conflict between the two – either in Europe or outside it – and the rise of a great variety of social policies has been observed lately.[7] The question is rather political, linked to the inherent dynamics of the Polanyian double movement.

IMBALANCES, DISORDER AND MIGRATION

Alongside growing inequalities under neoliberalism, in recent decades the world has also experienced migration dynamics of a hitherto

---

7   See Haggard and Kaufman (2020) and Ocampo and Stiglitz (2018).

unseen intensity, resulting from various military conflicts and situations of political instability in combination with the increasingly rapid communication attributable to globalization. Numerous European countries that previously tended to be the origins of international migration have now become its targets. Consequently, it is important to ask how migration impacts welfare systems.

Collier (2015) takes the view that migration weakens solidarity since it creates more heterogeneous societies, with commitment to welfare systems dwindling as a consequence. However, there are examples that contradict Collier's thesis. Migrants are in many cases net contributors to the welfare coffers of receiving countries, helping to make their systems sustainable. In addition, immigration may induce social policymakers to add new elements to the welfare systems of the receiving country. In this way, for example, the need for integration arising in the wake of immigration to the Netherlands engendered microloan schemes supported by the state (and the EU), as well as various forms of support for social enterprises in general. Within the EU, more intense internal migration also amplifies the need for common social regulation, meaning that shared norms tend to gain, rather than lose, strength. At the same time, following the long crisis in Europe there is both a need and an opportunity for reinforcement of social coordination. Globalization and global economic competition increasingly appear as incentives for this process, rather than counterarguments against it.

As economists and sociologists interpret it, migration is governed by a confluence of pull and push factors. Behind every large-scale migration is some significant imbalance, as well as a great many individual decisions. A variety of reasons for migration can be distinguished, but separating the migrants themselves into different groups is more problematic. It is difficult to define one immigrant as purely political, another as purely economic. In most cases, any combination of economic, professional, family, political, cultural, lifestyle and other factors can be at play in the choice to emigrate or immigrate, and these factors can act in combination not only within each individual but also within families.

Economic growth and high average incomes certainly exert an attractive pulling power towards certain countries, even if in those same countries unemployment sometimes rises or incomes decline within given periods. In recent decades, many people have moved from abroad to work in the United Kingdom and Germany (both from within the EU and from outside it), while both countries have been able to display growth above, and unemployment below, the EU average (at least before the start of the Brexit process). However, it must of course be acknowledged that Germany should have done more for the integration of Turkish immigrants, and the same can be said of the United Kingdom with respect to those arriving from the Commonwealth and other parts of the world.

Conversely, deep recessions push immigration back. Because of declining labour demand in the economies of Britain, Spain and other countries, the protracted economic crisis that began in 2007–8 held back, rather than increased, immigration to Europe. Immigration took place on a far greater scale in the years of prosperity leading up to the financial crash than in the years that followed. Clouding the picture further, we can also see that internal migration within the EU has picked up again in the intervening time (with increasing numbers migrating northwards from the deeply recession-hit Southern Europe), while immigration from outside the EU, having declined by around half following the crisis, has barely risen.

Alongside these quantitative changes, the nature of migration has also changed. In the wake of worsening and increasingly virulent conflicts in the Middle East and North Africa, as well as the militarization of the 2011 Arab Spring, refugees have come to represent a considerably greater proportion of overall migration. There are far more dispossessed individuals and families dwelling in temporary camps and requiring assistance as a humanitarian obligation. Of course, what might help the most is if order, political stability and the conditions for normal economic activity were to be restored in the countries of the region. For us to have to worry less about immigration, therefore, much could be achieved via foreign and security policy, as well as by the improvement of international economic relations.

After the refugee crisis of 2015, it became clear to many that the Dublin/Schengen model, which had been designed a quarter-century earlier for the regulation of asylum and free movement within the

Union, had passed its sell-by date. However, in order for it to be replaced by something new, EU institutions would need to conduct a deeper, broader dialogue with member states about the correlations between demographics, immigration and the European Neighbourhood Policy. Answers must be given to allay concerns over whether openness to migration burdens Europe with huge security risks or lays it open to terrorism. Since the terror attacks on Paris in 2015, one main topic of debate has been whether a link exists between immigration and terrorism. To go even further, some ask whether there is any benefit or need for immigration at all if it might – presumably – engender such risks.

First of all, it is necessary to clarify what factors actually drive terrorist acts – besides the requisite sizeable helping of human wickedness and hatred. According to American economist Jeffrey Sachs, the Islamist terrorism of recent decades is an extension of wars in the Middle East. Even by conservative estimates, the invasion and occupation of Iraq that began in 2003 claimed more than 100,000 civilian victims. As a consequence of the Syrian conflict – initiated by the United States and its allies to weaken Assad's patrons in Iran and Russia – around 200,000 have died and 3,700,000 have fled abroad. 'Ending the terror of radical Islam will require ending the West's wars for control in the Middle East. Fortunately, the Age of Oil is gradually coming to an end,' writes Sachs. Similarly, writing in the pages of *Foreign Policy*, Stephen Walt makes the connection between conflicts and interventions in the Middle East and the Paris terror attacks of 2015. In his view, American (and other western) interventions do not necessarily have to be seen as wrong or condemned in order for us to discover that the events in New York, Madrid and Paris had their roots in the imperial or other military interventions of the preceding period.

This connection becomes even clearer if, besides the examples given above and other recent cases such as those in Nice and Barcelona, we mention other incidences of terrorism from history. Across almost a century in Northern Ireland, for example, terror acts were perpetrated that obviously had nothing to do with immigration, while religion (setting Catholics against Protestants) was more of an identity-shaping factor alongside a more deeply rooted cause:

namely, the decline of the British Empire and the safeguarding of the geopolitical interests of the United Kingdom. Knowing all this, it seems clear that identifying immigration and immigrants with the threat of terrorism is useful only in diverting attention away from other problems and anomalies. In addition, such an identification is a gift for extremists, whose principal or ancillary preoccupation is to stir up suspicion and hatred and promote the exclusion of those with a different skin colour, religion or customs.

Xenophobic political discourse routinely drowns out voices declaring that immigrants are expressly needed in the European economy. We can regard this as a basic economic and demographic truth, for the simple reason that without immigration Europe's population will decline; indeed, even with immigration, the working-age population has already begun to decline. Although cultural differences can be important both within and outside Europe, the economic balance and solidarity between generations is just as important. According to Giles Merritt (2016), Europe is still failing to face up to the reality of its population stagnating and growing older, with the consequence that its share of the world's total population is progressively shrinking while its economic growth potential languishes below other, more dynamic regions. For these reasons, Europe has no choice but to pursue an active immigration policy and invest more in the integration of immigrants. This will eventually strengthen economic competitiveness, making it easier to overcome the social problems brought about by having an ageing population.

If a textbook existed for populist politicians, the tactic of pointing at immigrants and using them as scapegoats would appear in one of its first chapters. In many cases, populist manifestations of this kind are more powerful where there are fewer immigrants than in places where they are familiar: where people live, study and work with them. In the United Kingdom, for example, there was greater support for the UK Independence Party (and Brexit) outside of London. Similarly, in Germany some of the greatest antipathy towards poor immigrants has been in Bavaria, while in Switzerland people outside the major cities voted in larger numbers for restrictions on immigration when a referendum was held on the issue. At such times, suspicion and hostility towards immigrants is linked with aversion to change and with arguments over distribution quotas within countries.

The immigrant is the most easily deployable scapegoat in politics. Moreover, a xenophobic mood is easiest to whip up where leading figures in politics are unable – or unwilling – to provide another explanation for growing inequalities or the uncertainties of daily life. Imbalances in the global economy and changes in the international division of labour are in certain cases putting a strain not only on the welfare models of developed countries but on their political systems as well. This is particularly true where uneven development entails major deficits and relative decline; in other words, where losses, not profits, must be shared out within society. If a systemic correction of inequalities is not forthcoming, then the urgency of the situation may enforce chaotic, haphazard solutions that take the form of open or hidden conflicts.

THE EU IN THE VORTEX OF GLOBALIZATION

From a European perspective, it is important to make clear that both the first and second phases of globalization put the European welfare models to the test, either in terms of employment capacity or through the ability to finance social policy. The high degree of internationalization and deregulation in the modern global economy has undermined the strength of national governments, national labour movements and nation-based capital – all of which represent the typical participants in the consensus around national welfare states. Prolonged depressions have occurred in European regions where changes in outsourcing and the division of labour on a global scale have led to deindustrialization and long-term unemployment.

In the 1960s, the ratio of registered unemployed was around 3–4% in Europe and North America and 2% in Japan. Following some fluctuations, the official jobless rate in the early to mid 1990s had risen to more than 10% in the EU and to 7% in the United States while remaining extremely low in Japan. By 2003, however, it stood at 8% in the EU, 6.2% in the United States and 5.5% in Japan. The net effect, therefore, was a significant rise over several decades. Official unemployment statistics only register those actively seeking work, however, and an even better indicator is therefore the employment rate, which shows substantial declines in times of crisis.

Companies thinking in terms of global opportunities can easily relocate production to a country further away with much lower wage costs and fewer state regulations; this can significantly increase unemployment back at home, especially in industrialized areas. The more affluent strata of society can optimize their financial investments on a global scale, allowing them to soar ahead of the rest – even without accounting for the option of hiding their high earnings in tax havens. If the tax base narrows and workers' incomes stagnate, the public sector is also put under pressure (along with the working conditions and earning opportunities of its employees). The new global economic order has thus provided more options for capital than for labour: as the wage share has begun to decline in developed countries, unemployment has settled at consistently higher levels almost everywhere. It seems that a 'precariat' is emerging: a new class of people living in conditions of uncertainty.[8]

It is no wonder, therefore, that alarm bells have begun ringing over the sustainability of the welfare state as a consequence of the labour market transformations and social processes linked to globalization – in Northern and Southern, Eastern and Western Europe alike. This first occurred because of the slowdown in growth in the 1970s, when it became difficult to guarantee an improved standard of living for everyone amid conditions of stagflation. Subsequently, in the English-speaking world, the neoconservative Thatcher–Reagan counter-revolution declared an attack on the very notions of welfare redistribution and state intervention in the economy. The breakup of the Soviet Union then signified the disappearance of an important external incentive for western market economies to adopt models that were more socially oriented. Finally, by citing the economic successes of emerging countries and the competition they created, it was possible to eliminate benefits deemed unjustified or unsustainable from an economic perspective.

---

8   The precariat is a kind of lower working class whose members have lost their job security and the regulated working conditions and income stability that come with it. See Standing (2011).

Even if, in many cases, all this has led to an erosion rather than a collapse of the welfare state, this erosion and its associated affective experience have proven enduring. In the period of wars since 2001, and to an even greater extent following the Great Recession, a feeling of stability has been missing from the international environment as a whole, and we have talked instead of a new 'global economic disorder'. This feeling only intensified as the United States openly turned against the institutional system of multilateralism following the election of Donald Trump as president in 2016. This turnaround in Washington also created a new situation for the EU in its connection to global politics and economics. Alloying traditional Republican politics with elements of fascism, Trump shattered the historical consensus that had existed since World War II, whereby Washington had always been a proponent and supporter of Western European, and then pan-European, unity. The exit from the Paris Agreement and many other similar moves showed that the United States was no longer necessarily a stabilizing force; it instead tended to undermine hitherto existing forms of global cooperation.

There is no better – and from the EU's point of view, no more important – example of the destabilizing effect of neoliberal globalization than Brexit, or the departure of the United Kingdom from the EU that began following the referendum of 23 June 2016. Although Prime Minister David Cameron originally called the referendum in order to convince Brits of the wisdom of staying in the EU, a narrow but significant majority of the population (52% of those participating in the plebiscite) voted for Brexit. The result of the referendum did not come out of the blue: for many years, the British had operated as the most reluctant partners in the Union. This reluctance often hindered the optimal functioning of the EU as a whole. The UK political tabloid press has long been dominated by anti-European stereotypes; however, the majority of British citizens would not have opted to depart if it had not given them the opportunity to vote against a conservative elite that attempted to reduce EU membership to the bare bones of the free market, burdening wage-earners, local governments and stagnating parts of the country far from the prosperous capital with largely superfluous austerity measures.

Although the EU cannot be held responsible for the holding of the Brexit referendum, or for its result, there are a number of lessons to be drawn from this case. One is that more must be done within EU institutions – in the field of communications and beyond – to familiarize citizens with European integration and win it acceptance and appreciation. Where nationalist media is strong, the need for pro-EU resources and endeavours is especially great. More important, however, is to provide a better outline of the economic benefits of EU membership, and this cannot be entrusted exclusively to national governments. As well as being strengthened, the tools that Europe can use to mitigate the risks and harms of globalization also need to be made more visible.

The EU itself was at the vanguard of the globalization process, but it created only a single tool to defend against its negative effects – the European Globalisation Adjustment Fund (EGF) – and it did so only in 2006. This tool offers the opportunity for workers who were displaced in large numbers as a consequence of the changing international division of labour to receive support from EU funds. The EGF nevertheless remains insufficient to forestall sudden changes of this kind, or to reverse the changes that have led to deindustrialization – and relative impoverishment – in previously prosperous regions (such as Northern England, Wallonia and Galicia). Moreover, use of the EGF is made more difficult by the fact that it does not have its own budget, and that it is not available in cases where the number of those affected by job losses due to changes in the international division of labour does not exceed a minimum level. (This level was originally set at 500 people, but it was then reduced to 250 in the seven-year budget beginning in 2021.)

Beyond the EGF, there are other examples that reveal that in Europe it is no longer nation states but the EU that provides a strong framework to restrict the excessive power of multinational corporations. Within this EU framework, it is competition policy that provides the tools to stand up against abuses by companies such as Microsoft and Gazprom. Though the procedure took many years, the European Commission did eventually fine Google close to €2.5 billion for distortion of competition. All these are important instruments for transforming a business model that concentrates profits within a narrow circle while leaving multitudes of workers and consumers at the mercy of corporations.

In 2017, the European Commission issued a discussion paper that looked into how the energies of globalization might be put into the service of economic prosperity in Europe. This led to the launch of legislative work aimed at enforcing European social norms within global supply chains. All these EU policies hark back to the social democratic programme promoted in the latter phase of the Cold War by Willy Brandt, Olof Palme and Gro Harlem Brundtland. These politicians, at the head of various UN committees, engaged with questions of international development, the management of global tensions, and ecological and social sustainability. It is thanks to them that the tasks of resolving the ecological crisis and creating a more equitable international economic order have become the guiding motivations of social democracy, but they have also exercised an influence on other trends, as they recognized that the preservation of Europe's achievements in welfare is closely related to the evolution of the global economic order. Social democrats do not regard globalization as a calamity, but they do reject its neoliberal form. As the Australian economist Bill Mitchell puts it: 'Globalisation mixed with neo-liberalism is poison. Globalisation mixed with social democracy is progress.' In practice, this would mean that the principles of democratic, social and environmental policy must be taken into account in every decision that has an impact on global economic relations.[9]

---

9   An example of this was furnished at the end of 2016 by Paul Magnette, then Socialist minister-president of Wallonia, when for precisely these reasons he held up the signing of a trade agreement due to be concluded between the EU and Canada. His positions are laid out in the so-called Namur Declaration.

Currency, crisis, solidarity

MONETARY UNION: POLITICS DOMINATES

Prior to bowing out as president of the European Commission in 2014, José Manuel Barroso gave a lecture at Humboldt University of Berlin in which he outlined five main tasks to pursue. Listed first among these was the strengthening of Economic and Monetary Union (EMU). Based on the experiences of his second term as president, Barroso had every reason to declare this as the most important issue on the European Union's agenda: if the tension between the centre and the periphery within the eurozone could not be relieved within a short period of time, then a fresh crisis might once again call into question not only the survival of the euro but the very stability of the EU as a whole.

Over the past thirty years, the euro has been not only a financial project but additionally – and perhaps even primarily – a political one. In the latter capacity, its mission is to integrate the continent as a whole, naturally with the concomitant imperative of promoting its economic prosperity. However, the global financial crisis served to highlight that in its original form (based on the blueprint drawn up at the beginning of the 1990s) the euro is unable to fulfil either its economic or its political function.

It is the mission of the EU to eliminate dangerous divisions on the continent, transcending the nationalist tendencies that threaten to pull its peoples apart. Such divisions have led to innumerable conflicts over the centuries. European integration has built its manifesto for peace using economic tools, one of these being the creation of a common currency. But how far the euro is able to fulfil its uniting function as the EU's common currency remains an open question.

The projection of European monetary integration into the political sphere is above all about the relationship between Germany and France. One immediate preliminary to the inclusion of EMU as an objective in the Maastricht Treaty was German reunification, to which France's leaders only agreed on the condition that the Germans renounced their national currency. However, the project did not appear out of thin air, since earlier phases of monetary cooperation had already arisen, based on a clear economic concept with the aim of ensuring the price stability needed for the expansion of European trade.

After US President Richard Nixon cancelled the dollar's convertibility to gold in 1971, thereby removing the American currency from its function as an aid to global price stability, European countries had to work out for themselves how to filter out price movements that were detrimental to international trade and investment. The initial steps were aided by the favourable rapport that evolved in the 1970s between Valéry Giscard d'Estaing and Helmut Schmidt. Initially as finance ministers, and then as French president and German chancellor, respectively, the pair worked together to create the European Monetary System (EMS). The Maastricht Treaty, and with it the creation of the EU itself, was then brought about by the other major pairing of François Mitterrand and Helmut Kohl.

The initial model of EMU, which was maintained right up until the global financial crisis, was framed by the Maastricht Treaty, signed in 1992. This was the outcome of a quarter-century-long series of developments – essentially starting from the breakup of the Bretton Woods monetary system – that brought the EU to the beginning of the process of the abolition of national currencies. Jacques Delors, the then president of the European Commission, entrusted the preparation of the technicalities of currency union in the Treaty to a committee of central bank governors. With the embryonic EMU model, the central bankers succeeded in eliminating a potential recurrence of the currency crises that had previously afflicted Europe. However, by ruling out devaluation, and in the absence of other equalizing mechanisms, the likelihood of fiscal and social crises simultaneously increased.

Overall, from the early 1990s monetary cooperation among EU countries proceeded more rapidly than cooperation in other areas, largely for political reasons that saw the euro's unifying function placed front and centre. The euro was introduced as the common currency, albeit without an EU-level supervisory system to oversee financial institutions operating in the single market; without proper economic governance to help maintain balanced growth; and without a unified, solid crisis management mechanism in the event of shocks.

EU experts have good reason to regard Jacques Delors as an outstanding Commission president. However, he strengthened only the single market's social dimension, and not that of its currency union. The distinction between the two is very important indeed. While earlier, in the 1970s, a number of documents were prepared envisaging monetary union in tandem with a regime of substantive fiscal instruments (e.g. a common unemployment benefit scheme), this aspect was entirely absent from the Maastricht concept. We may thus speak of a kind of Delors paradox: although the social legislation Delors initiated in relation to the single market carries great significance, its effectiveness is undermined by the operation of the currency union that was also shaped by Delors, which causes social polarization rather than unification.

When the euro was introduced as legal tender, Gerhard Schröder and Jacques Chirac held office in Berlin and Paris, respectively. But it did not fall to them to confront new problems and take on the tasks of crisis management. That was the responsibility of the leaders who followed them – Angela Merkel and Nicolas Sarkozy – who had to face the difficult task of holding together the currency union at the start of the global economic crisis (2008–9) and during the subsequent eurozone crisis. Although the French–German axis did not topple over in either the Merkel–Sarkozy or Merkel–Hollande periods, increasingly obvious differences of opinion emerged that rendered crisis management – and reforms aimed at sustaining the euro in the long term – progressively more difficult.[1]

---

1   As Brunnermeier, Landau and James (2016) put it, while Germany tends to regard the EMU more as a stability union, France attaches at least as much importance to growth and solidarity; in the event of crises, the French are more likely to support a recovery policy relying on common instruments. Groups of German and French economists (the Glienicker Group and the Eiffel Group) endeavoured to promote convergence in economic strategy between the two countries in the years following the global crisis.

It is no exaggeration to say that the eurozone was facing the imminent possibility of disintegration in 2011–12. The new president of the European Central Bank (ECB), Mario Draghi, prevented the worst-case scenario in July 2012 when he announced that he would do whatever it took to preserve the common currency. In the years that followed, the eurozone extricated itself from its serious crisis, and it began the reform of EMU, but the speed of the reforms proved insufficient to consolidate the system for the long term. While the EU won some time, much more was required to achieve sustainability.

Almost immediately after being elected president of France in 2017, Emmanuel Macron presented his programme for reinforcing European integration. The first official trip of the former presidential advisor and economy minister was to Berlin to draw up a joint agenda for the further reform of the EU, and most importantly of the euro. Although there have often been attempts to count France among Europe's ailing economies, it was clear that Macron had not travelled to Berlin for economic assistance. The performance of the French economy barely lagged behind that of Germany's, and France's national debt was scarcely more than Germany's. France needed the euro to become a political success, and to that end it proposed substantial reforms on Germany's part to reduce divergence in the eurozone (as discussed later in the chapter). Essentially, the EU's old model would need to be changed once again, to adjust to the disparate specific characteristics of the countries making up the eurozone.

THE EUROZONE'S CENTRE AND PERIPHERY

The EU has of course never been a homogeneous system. It has become progressively more diverse with each successive expansion, and in many respects the global financial crisis only exacerbated the differences, creating new asymmetries. Now, however, it is a matter not merely of diversity but also of divergence and of significant inequalities that may eventually pull the entire system apart. It is for this reason that the concept of uneven development and the dual notion of the centre and the periphery are applicable in describing the processes and structural asymmetries within the EU.

The dynamics of historical development in the context of European integration are determined by the deepening tendency of the market and the gradual improvement of equalizing mechanisms.[2] The evolution of the common or single internal market within the EU brought about an expansion and strengthening of the elements of cohesion policy (such as support for developmental investments through a common budget). However, the Maastricht model failed to take into account the fact that monetary union – via its unintended consequences in the form of the fragmentation of the financial sector – would have an even stronger polarizing impact than the single market. This raises the need for an additional equalizing mechanism if sustainability and optimal operation are to be guaranteed. The lack of such equalization is apparent primarily, though not exclusively, in the social dimension of currency union.

Polarization reveals the EU's diversity, its social and cultural differences, and the formation and coexistence of divergent models of capitalism. However, more important than the distinctions between north and south, Protestant and Catholic, or nations that drink beer and those that drink wine is the way in which trade and capital movements (deficits and surpluses) shape the relationship between the centre and the periphery within the EU economy.

What I call the periphery in the EU context is more properly a semi-periphery when viewed in the context of the global economy. Its income level is considerably higher than the average for the global economy, it may fulfil the functions of a 'centre' in relation to certain alternative regions (see the Ibero–Latin American relationship), and it may join with the elite that governs global affairs (as in the case of Italy and the G7). Based on the economic processes that constitute the EU's operations, however, we can indeed speak of peripheral countries or regions (which are not necessarily southern, since Latvia and Ireland, for example, are also considered part of the periphery).

---

2   Sociological research into these dynamics of development may find Karl Polanyi's theory of the 'double movement' to be invaluable, thus proving its legitimacy.

The crisis in the southern periphery was essentially foreseen by the Belgian economist André Sapir, who – further elaborating on Esping-Andersen's typology – distinguished four social models within Europe (see Table 2).

Table 2. Efficiency vs. equity (André Sapir's classification).

		Efficiency	
		High	**Low**
Equity	**High**	Continentals (Germany, France, Netherlands, Austria)	Nordics (Sweden, Finland, Norway, Denmark)
	Low	Mediterraneans (Italy, Spain, Portugal, Greece)	Anglo-Saxons (United Kingdom, Ireland)

Fundamentally, all Sapir did was to detach the social models of Mediterranean countries from the continental or 'Rhine' model on the basis of factors such as less efficient public administration or weaker conciliation of competing interests. The Scandinavian model was classified as efficient and equitable, while the Mediterranean model was declared quite the opposite – and with that, Sapir pronounced the Southern European models unsustainable.

At the time of the 2010–13 eurozone crisis, a marked divergence became apparent between north and south (or, more precisely, between the centre and the periphery of the zone), starting with financial fragmentation and continuing with a protracted southern recession, asymmetric growth in unemployment and poverty, and the emergence of divergent political paradigms. Substantial reform of EMU would have been needed for renewed convergence (indeed, even before the crisis): as Aidan Regan (2015) and others have noted, EMU melded together several economic governance models in such a way that it eliminated the demand-stimulating tools that the countries of the periphery were traditionally able to utilize while offering nothing else to take their place.

During the crisis, the countries of the periphery made continuous efforts – with EU assistance – to stimulate investment, job creation and growth, although these efforts in themselves were able to contribute only in small measure to recovery. While the more effective mobilization of EU funds is important, it does not in itself generate more funding. The elaboration of novel financial solutions (such as project bonds) is promising, but their realization needs time, as well as a greater degree of institutional innovation than has previously been seen (such as the creation of a European investment agency). Although structural reforms in areas such as labour markets and pensions have been an ongoing concern in Southern Europe, they more tend to improve long-term growth potential than to generate short-term upswings.

In the period 2011–12 the fear of the disintegration of the eurozone, combined with the threat of the exclusion of certain countries, deepened the crisis just as much as the financial fragmentation typifying the private sector did, or capital flight from countries on the brink of bankruptcy. But how did this vicious circle come to evolve in Europe?

The stereotypical interpretation of the eurozone crisis holds that the southern states were spending beyond their means; the reason for their woes was that they had broken the rules, particularly the budget deficit threshold of 3% of GDP. In reality, Spain kept to all existing rules, while infringement of the Maastricht criteria was likewise not the main problem in either Italy or Portugal. Although all the countries concerned committed errors to a greater or lesser extent – with Greece's budget really failing to meet required norms – the regional imbalances were caused primarily by unregulated flows of capital from the centre to the periphery, and by the lack of preparedness on the part of the EU as a whole for managing the resultant crisis.

The Maastricht structure of European currency union went far beyond the level of integration of the European Monetary System (EMS) that functioned in the 1980s, since it eliminated national currencies and created the ECB. Nevertheless, this historic leap did not immediately close the gap between form and content, given that the operating logic of the system scarcely goes beyond the mechanism known as a currency board. Its designers (members of the one-time Delors Committee) underestimated the impact of a lack of flexible or adjustable exchange rates, while at the same time overestimating the EU's ability to introduce missing elements of EMU during transition periods in a preventive way ahead of still greater crises.

The conclusion that the eurozone is not an optimal currency area (to use an expression of Robert Mundell[3]) seems a euphemistic description of the situation. One conspicuous consequence of the eurozone crisis has been the upsurge in intra-European migration, and the changing character and direction of this migration. Many people migrated to other countries of the EU (e.g. to Germany, with its continuously high level of demand), but many also went to other continents: the Portuguese to Brazil, the Greeks to Australia, and the Irish to North America. The more highly educated have been over-represented among these migrants, leading to a possibly lasting loss of human capital in the affected countries and a consequent reduction in their growth potential.

EMU CRISIS AND SOCIAL DIVERGENCE

The EU (and the eurozone within it) is heterogeneous: it unites a disparate set of business and social models. To achieve the cohesion established as a goal in the EU treaties, it is important to ensure that the social and economic advancement of the EU periphery is more dynamic and conspicuous than that of the semi-periphery of the global economy in general.[4] However, the Maastricht model was born in a period when faith in the self-regulating capacity of markets was strong, and when it may have seemed that an institutional solution to guarantee money market equilibrium and fiscal prudence within the EU was not needed. Later corrective measures, aimed at strengthening financial stability or economic governance, were insufficiently vigorous to move beyond the confines of the model. European society has paid a heavy price in recent years for the design errors committed a quarter of a century ago.

---

3   Mundell was a Nobel Prize-winning Canadian economist and professor at New York's Columbia University. He originated the hypothesis of the 'impossible trinity', whereby it is impossible to simultaneously apply a fixed exchange rate, pursue an autonomous monetary policy and maintain the free movement of capital. Of the three criteria, only two at most may prevail at once.

4   I speak of 'social and economic advancement' because GDP is not everything: when evaluating progress, we must take into account a more complex set of social indicators, and the factors of the environment and quality of life.

Despite the EU placing ever-increasing emphasis on the social dimension and the importance of 'inclusive growth' in the period of the Europe 2020 Strategy, the financial and economic crisis that unfolded alongside it caused serious damage, setting back the progress that had been previously achieved in a number of countries. In 2010 the EU declared that the employment rate needed to be raised to 75% within ten years, and that the number of people living in poverty and exclusion needed to be reduced by 20 million from the 2008 level (the last year preceding the crisis). EU decision makers at the time regarded these as ambitious but realistic goals; at the same time, many people in 2010 – mainly those who were part of civil organizations – declared that these goals were not ambitious enough. Two years later, however, when the region had plunged into the eurozone crisis, the verdict was that the goal of reducing poverty was not realistic after all.

The unfolding of the eurozone crisis during the period 2010–11 cast the EU economy's dynamics adrift from other developed regions. While the United States and Japan had begun to recover following the recession of 2008–9, the EU sank into the depths of a renewed crisis. The primary reason for this was the deficient structure of EMU, which lacked the kind of instruments that could have been used to simultaneously lend assistance to countries losing the option of market financing and sustain the economic upturn that had begun in 2010. The internal imbalances and the inadequate toolbox of the eurozone led to the emergence of a second European recession (2011–13) within the decade-long financial crisis. This only further exacerbated the existing asymmetries within the eurozone, setting the financially stronger, surplus-producing centre against the more exposed and helpless periphery.

The centre officially became the periphery's creditor, which led to political polarization on top of the financial imbalances while at the same time making it harder to objectively seek solutions that would enable the impasse to be resolved. Without the option of devaluation of national currencies, and in the absence of transfers to put a brake on the decline, the periphery has been forced to rely on what is known as internal devaluation. This means cutting back wages and public expenditures, on the assumption that these measures will restore the given economy's competitiveness and growth potential, and consequently the financial standing of the state.

Internal devaluation thus stood in for currency devaluation, but it proved a poor substitute in every respect. On the one hand, it was economically inadequate, since if internal devaluation is applied by several countries at once, then instead of restoring competitiveness it narrows aggregate demand within the currency union, and it thus deepens the recession rather than triggering a recovery. And on the other hand, it is also a bad substitute in the social sense, since it increases unemployment, poverty and inequality considerably more than currency devaluation (which also immediately devalues assets). The net result is that the polarization between the more developed economies and the less developed ones within the eurozone has become far more pronounced than the polarization that prevails between the countries outside it.

In the years and decades before the crisis, convergence between the EU's centre and its periphery was evident not only in the GDPs of national economies but also in employment and social indicators. After 2008, and the start of the crisis, a divergence could be observed instead. With regard to the three key indicators of the effectiveness of welfare systems – levels of unemployment, poverty and inequality – it can be said that, as a consequence of the crisis, the diversity that was characteristic of the EU as a whole gave way to divergence within the eurozone.

As far as the unemployment rate is concerned, the EU member states were characterized by polarization to an unprecedented degree during the prolonged crisis period (from 2008 right up until 2013). The fact that unemployment levels rise during an economic crisis is not extraordinary in itself; what was extraordinary in this case was the scale of the rise, and more importantly that it was not distributed evenly but instead reflected the financial and economic positions of individual countries or groups of countries. At the EU level, unemployment increased almost continuously from 2008 onwards (except for a short pause in 2010–11), peaking at 11% in 2013 (12% in the eurozone). Youth unemployment (the jobless rate among those aged 25 and under) rose practically uninterruptedly during the same period. It is at least as important to highlight, however, that the course of unemployment followed the contours of financial and economic polarization, meaning that it essentially stagnated in the core countries of the eurozone (even steadily decreasing in Germany) while scaling record heights in the peripheral eurozone countries. In the two hardest-hit countries – Spain and Greece – the jobless rate peaked at more than 25%, and youth unemployment in both countries peaked at more than 50%.

The polarization that occurred in unemployment rates is also an important development because the decade preceding the crisis was characterized by convergence. The bursting of financial bubbles and the Great Recession of 2009, followed by various financial stabilization programmes, nevertheless clearly hit the countries of the periphery hard. There, the crisis in the real economy was deeper and more prolonged, while fiscal consolidation had a negative impact on both wages and the standard of social provision.

Similar asymmetries also characterized the tendencies of poverty and social exclusion. In the two largest economies of the eurozone – Germany and France – together with Belgium, poverty and social exclusion largely stagnated, while in some countries they even decreased despite the crisis. This latter group contained both 'eastern' and 'western' countries (Austria, Romania, the Czech Republic and Finland). At the same time, the eurozone periphery – and above all the countries of Southern Europe – experienced a significant increase in poverty and social exclusion between 2008 and 2013.

In contrast to the unemployment rate, the fiscal capacity of individual countries, or their 'automatic stabilizers', played a key role in the evolution of poverty. Two phases of the prolonged crisis should be clearly distinguished in this regard. In the first phase of the crisis (2008–10), the budgetary stabilizers of EU member states functioned well and the population's freely disposable income did not track the decline in the economy and employment levels. By contrast, in the second phase (the eurozone crisis between 2011 and 2013), budgetary room for manoeuvre narrowed and – partly due to new and stricter fiscal rules – the automatic stabilizers could not bring their impact to bear and household incomes decreased over a prolonged period. Therefore, despite the fact that the economic decline in the period 2011–13 was not as steep as it was in 2009, social conditions on average deteriorated to a more significant extent.

In terms of income inequality (as measured by the Gini index), the EU member states display substantial differences – it would be difficult to demonstrate a uniform European model. In different countries and for completely different reasons, income inequality can be high (as in the United Kingdom and Latvia) or comparatively low (Austria and Slovakia). Greece and Spain stand out, in that inequality in these countries was already among the highest prior to the crisis and only widened further as a consequence of it.

The divergence between the centre and the periphery of the eurozone is well demonstrated by the Social Scoreboard introduced by the European Commission in 2013.[5] With this it is possible to trace the width of the divide between the core and peripheral countries with respect to indicators such as the jobless rate or income inequality. Social imbalances are demonstrable in the case of almost all indicators, but they are most striking when it comes to unemployment.

Social asymmetries between the centre and periphery have also been demonstrated by Tito Boeri (2015), who conducted a 'stress test' of welfare systems based on a database from the crisis period. According to Boeri:

> It turns out that for the European Union as a whole, a recession which results in a drop of 0.7 per cent of GDP will significantly increase the poverty rate. However, there is a large variation between EU countries. Whereas in some Southern European countries even a milder recession will increase poverty rates, in the Nordic countries a recession as high as 5 per cent of GDP does not result in a rise in poverty rates. This underlines that there are substantial differences in the way in which different countries in Europe react to these conditions.
>
> Similar findings come from analysing the poverty rates and unemployment rates. In Southern Europe it is sufficient to have a rise in unemployment of around 1.3 base points for poverty to

---

5   The five indicators were unemployment, youth unemployment, the NEET rate, income inequality measured with the S80/S20 formula and relative poverty. The scoreboard was introduced in the Commission's 2013 communication on EMU's social dimension, which it later revised and expanded in the context of the 2017 Social Pillar.

increase, while in the Nordic countries the relation between poverty rates and unemployment is almost flat: unemployment can rise
significantly without affecting poverty. So clearly there is a problem
of vulnerability in certain parts of Europe which does not exist in
other countries to the same extent.

HOW MANY PRESIDENTS DOES IT TAKE?

Since 2012, numerous EU documents have determined that the solution to the crisis of the euro is closer cooperation, meaning a shift
towards banking union, fiscal union and political union. The most
important of these documents was the Four Presidents' Report,[6]
completed in 2012, with which EU leaders opened a new chapter by
announcing a comprehensive plan to deepen and sustain EMU. This
vision – to which the European Commission, also in 2012, attached
a detailed schedule under the title of 'Blueprint' – includes a wide
range of proposed tools with the potential to perfect the system.
However, currency reform continued to make only halting progress
because leading politicians – with an eye on the 2014 elections for
the European Parliament – did not sense citizens' support for the
introduction of these new tools, while procrastination over reforms
naturally eroded confidence in integration, which was already low
given the continuing period of weak economic performance.

Initially (in the period 2010–12), the question of EMU reform
was mostly a debate between two poles: one urged more rapid progress, while the other wanted a deceleration or even a retreat (e.g. by
doing away with the European Stability Mechanism (ESM)). A
third position later took shape in this debate, which held that the
elements of fiscal union were not necessary for a break with the
earlier, austerity-based crisis management strategy. One side (the
south) should relinquish its claim for transfers, while the other
(the north) should abandon rigid fiscal rules. In other words, the

---

6   The authors were President of the European Council Herman Van Rompuy,
President of the European Commission José Manuel Barroso, President of
the European Central Bank Mario Draghi and President of the Eurogroup
Jean-Claude Juncker.

solution would be a 'renationalization' of fiscal policy through a restoration of the 'no bail-out' rule, backed up by a sovereign debt restructuring mechanism.

The majority of economists – even, perhaps, in Germany – would agree that various solidarity instruments would be needed to create a more rapidly growing, more balanced eurozone under its current composition. However, there are those in Berlin, the Hague, Helsinki and other places besides who believe that, if the present model does not suit everybody, then the weak should get out. If, however, this were to apply not only to Greece but also, as it most likely would, to larger countries (all the way up to Italy), then the European character of the common currency would evaporate – and the proposition that the euro serves the EU's economic and political unity would prove untenable.

Joseph Stiglitz's book on the euro,[7] published in 2016, leaves no doubt that sweeping reforms are needed in today's European Union, primarily in order to restore the viability of currency union. The Nobel-winning economist claims – unsurprisingly, given his previous work – that the main problem with the EU is currency union itself – or, more precisely, the specific model used. A quarter of a century ago, the politicians who founded the EU were careless in making the erroneous assumption that the replacement of national currencies with a common one would carry the Union forward. Not only did this not eventuate, but the Union became even more divided, unstable and polarized than had a common currency not been introduced.

The euro has clearly been in crisis since 2010, which has not only distressed the members of the eurozone but also helped to discourage the British – who kept their national currency – from even retaining their membership of the EU. Stiglitz believes that the EU is salvageable, but only via a fundamental reform of the euro, which in its

---

7   Stiglitz (2016) summarizes many years of criticism in his book on the euro. Many other American economists could be mentioned who have consistently cast doubt over the original model of the euro and its sustainability, such as Paul Krugman, Barry Eichengreen and James K. Galbraith. Australian economist Bill Mitchell (2015) attributes the failure to design a viable monetary union and reform it in time to 'groupthink' within EU institutions.

current form cannot be saved. Numerous tools should be used to strengthen currency union and thereby make it viable, from common bond issues to stronger common industrial policy. A significant portion of these proposals have featured in various EU documents, but essentially only banking union and the ESM actually embarked along the path to fruition – with the latter routinely mentioned as something that might give birth to a European Monetary Fund.

The number of possible solutions to the euro crisis is not infinite, and this also places limits on the number and concrete nature of scenarios for the future of the EU as a whole. The euro as a unified currency has its own economic logic, and this restricts the range of available options. If we wish to retain the common currency, then reform is needed, and this means the introduction of additional common tools in the eurozone. A decisive majority of European experts now essentially agree with Stiglitz, among them even many Germans (such as the members of the Glienicker Group).

Further hampering progress is the fact that the reform of the euro (often referred to as the 'deepening of the eurozone') may intensify antagonism between the old member countries and the new ones, and between those inside and outside the eurozone. As a consequence of reform of the eurozone (more precisely, of EMU), the creation of some form of fiscal capacity via a eurozone budget will sooner or later appear on the agenda. Either this will be embedded in the EU budget or it will be created outside of it, but whichever form it takes it may result in a reduction in the traditional levels of cohesion funding. Because of this, the antagonism surrounding fiscal interests may become one of the primary EU debates of the coming period, even if it is not directly connected to the proclamation of a 'two-speed' or 'multi-speed' EU.

Since the outbreak of the crisis, the countries of both the centre and the periphery have seen the emergence of voices and political forces calling for a return to the system of national currencies. However, the mainstream political parties uniformly take the view that any change to correct the inherited model must not call into question the existing integration, and indeed must deepen and complete it. There are many arguments against a reversal, fragmentation or withdrawal back to a national framework. Such arguments include the financial and economic cost of the potential discontinuation of the euro, society's demand for free movement within Europe, and Europe's steadily dwindling relative weight within the global economy. Despite the crisis, the euro has preserved its popularity and allure, illustrated – among other things – by the fact that even in hard times the expansion of the eurozone has continued smoothly, typically with the accession of relatively small new member states.

Comparative popularity, however, is not synonymous with sustainability of the status quo. A long-term solution to the euro crisis needs to be found at the systemic level, restoring every member country's growth potential and the possibility of convergence within the currency union. At the same time, systemic problems cannot be resolved merely through efforts at the level of member states – this much, at least, must certainly be distilled from the upheaval of 2011–12.

The readiness of the south for reform must be coupled with a willingness on the part of the north to provide support. New ties and new forms of cooperation are required, and above all there must be a restored conviction that each member state will gain most from cooperating with others. The Dutch and the Finns must sense a common community with the Spanish and the Greeks; the Swedes and the Belgians must realize the importance of solidarity with the Romanians and the Bulgarians – and vice versa.

A redesign of EMU is no mere 'technical' task. Neither model-building nor economic governance can be conceived in terms of technocratic activity. More needs to be done for social dialogue, for a more active civil society, and for understanding and cohesion between nations and cultures. Reform does not mean that EU cooperation should expand to new regions as an end in itself under the slogan of 'more Europe'. Instead, it means eliminating severe anomalies in the already-existing system of the common currency and fixing systemic faults.

One of the key elements of the EMU reform programme – the previously discussed banking union – remained active during the five-year Juncker cycle. A consensus was reached that bank crises similar to the most recent one should not develop in the future (with the help of a more robust Single Supervisory Mechanism), while settlement in the event of disruption should take place without burdening taxpayers or the budgets of member states (with the help of a Single Resolution Mechanism). However, banking union was merely the beginning – and certainly not the end – of EMU reform.

Juncker's presidency also saw the publication of the Five Presidents' Report, which took note of the previous momentum while emphasizing the inherent dangers of divergence for the community in general. The document plainly represents a symbol of what Claus Offe asserted in 2015: Europe has fallen into a trap. While it can no longer retreat from the level of integration already achieved, it lacks the sufficient momentum or political capital to move forward. The Juncker Commission's Five Presidents' Report and the 2017 White Paper on the EU's future were followed by a Reflection Paper, and analysis of both the obvious faults of EMU and the hidden ones has continued within expert circles – along with a search for solutions.

FISCAL CAPACITY FOR THE EUROZONE

So what comes next after banking union? Fundamentally we need to address two important courses of action. The first is a reconsideration of the mandate of the ECB, confirming its status as a lender of last resort and also clarifying once and for all what the ECB can and cannot do (not least to avoid recurring legal challenges whenever it acts in defence of the integrity of the single currency). The second is to begin building a common fiscal capacity.

There are numerous justifications for doing the latter, but the most important is that the inherited model, even after the implementation of banking union, is not fully resilient when it comes to coping with the impact of economic cycles or the internal asymmetries and imbalances of the eurozone. Indeed, these two problems tend to be mutually reinforcing, in the manner of a vicious circle. Although many balk at the concept of 'transfers', they are unavoidable in an integrated economic system. If the EU wishes to be a single market, then the higher-income countries must help the lower-income countries by allocating investment funds. Within the currency union (where the option of currency revaluation or devaluation is removed), those with a surplus must help countries suffering a deficit, striving as much as possible to ensure that the support goes to the most vulnerable and defenceless groups in the latter camp. In the ideal scenario, the instruments to guarantee all this would be at the ready before the next economic crisis hits.

If we examine only the economic arguments, it is clear that the creation of a fiscal capacity within the EMU framework would bring significant economic advantages to all. Although cyclical downturns would not be eliminated, and naturally these may still develop in the future, occasional recessions would be much milder and less destructive. Citizens, meanwhile, would feel that the EU is not there simply to set rules and tasks for them, but also to provide concrete financial assistance when the need is greatest. The success of currency reform is also in the interests of countries that are still outside the eurozone (since their future accession may prove easier if the eurozone functions more efficiently).

The election of Emmanuel Macron as France's president gave fresh impetus to the debate over fiscal reform, which by that time had expanded from expert circles to the political arena. As soon as he entered office, the young French president travelled to Berlin to discuss the timetable for reforms. Perhaps more than anyone, France needed the euro to be a political success, and for this to happen, two things were required. Firstly, Germany would have to work off its huge external economic surplus via increased investment and higher wages, creating greater aggregate demand in the eurozone. Secondly, Germany would also have to contribute to new fiscal instruments (put simply: transfers), of which the primary beneficiaries would be not the French but the countries of the southern periphery plus Ireland and the Baltic states.

If the breakup of the eurozone – or the risk thereof – is to be avoided, the most pressing questions may relate to the completion of banking union (with the introduction of deposit insurance) and the installation of fiscal stabilizers to aid risk sharing and convergence. If, with the strengthening of the euro, the EU should happen to become 'two-speed', then every country will decide for itself which of the Union's circles it belongs to. But if a country decides to take its place in the outer circle, then it will not hinder the inner circle's integrative efforts. In theory, but perhaps also in practice, Brexit may make it easier for the EU to adopt the reforms that are needed to strengthen cohesion among the remaining twenty-seven member states, and in particular among the countries of the eurozone.

The fact that the European Commission, in its long-term draft budget for 2021–7 published in May 2018, initiated the creation of a fiscal capacity for the eurozone might have appeared advantageous, but the size and nature of the specific proposal meant that it could be regarded more as a merely symbolic step, rightly termed by the *Financial Times* columnist Wolfgang Munchau as a homeopathic tool, bringing little benefit while possibly supplanting part of the traditional cohesion budget.

Until that point, the EU budget had had little to do with the monetary side of integration. For a long time – starting from the 1992 Maastricht Treaty enabling the introduction of the common currency – the concept held that currency union would not precipitate fiscal union, and for this reason no new budgetary tools were required. This proposition proved false – at least on the theoretical plane – in 2012, when the presidents of the European Council, the European Commission, the European Central Bank and the Eurogroup released their report into the deepening of EMU, in which they spoke of the necessity not only of banking union but also of fiscal union.

In the eight years that passed between 2012 and 2020, banking union was partly realized, the EU escaped from recession, and the third (and last) Greek financial rescue operation was completed. As far as fiscal union was concerned, however, no concrete (i.e. political) steps were taken, while a vast amount of analysis and debate was devoted to risk sharing and potential budgetary tools. The opportunity to take the initiative came in 2018 when the new seven-year budget of the EU was designed and the European Commission linked the question of EMU fiscal capacity to negotiation of the new Multiannual Financial Framework (MFF) that would come into effect after 2020.

The 2018 MFF proposal contained a programme with a price tag of €25 billion for support of economic reforms within member states (the Reform Support Programme), and it mentioned that the substance of the reforms will be guided by the recommendations of the European Semester. This was problematic for two reasons. On the one hand, the difficult situations related to currency union that might warrant community support are not primarily of a structural nature but relate more to economic and financial cycles. This is to say that it is not central support of structural reforms that is primarily lacking from the system but measures to offset fluctuating confidence in money markets and demand on the macroeconomic level. On the other hand, even if the content of structural reforms can be successfully determined, it is unlikely that these reforms can be uniformly priced and uniformly applied from Finland to Portugal, Ireland to Bulgaria.

The other instrument that was featured in the 2018 MFF proposal was the European Investment Stabilisation Function, designed to help continuity of investments and carrying a maximum price tag of €30 billion. However, rather than being a transfer this would have been a credit line for financing rising interest payments in times of crisis. Although this idea may have served a genuinely useful function, here too question marks abound. During a major crisis, the rescheduling of investments certainly enters the agenda, and requires time. Individual economic actors may transform in the meantime, or even disappear. On the other hand, investment support, though it may save a few prominent projects, is likely to be concentrated in certain territories, thereby offering asymmetric assistance within the given member country. Consideration thus needs to be given to which state functions should be entitled to support from a stabilization fund of this kind, as well as to how useful such a function can be without actual transfers.

Altogether, 'the mountain that laboured brought forth a mouse' could be a summary of Jean-Claude Juncker's budgetary proposals regarding eurozone fiscal capacity. Or, to use another image, the Commission failed to repair the roof when the sun was shining: despite having produced valuable analytical and policy documents – in particular the reports from 2012 that revealed the nature of the crisis and the scale of reforms needed – they subsequently lacked the necessary political support to move ahead in the spirit of those revelations.

THE LONG ROAD TO UNEMPLOYMENT INSURANCE

It was one of the most counter-intuitive developments in the history of European economic policy when, in 2018, the then finance minister of Germany, Olaf Scholz,[8] spoke supportively of the concept of unemployment insurance in an interview with *Der Spiegel* – a view he continued to adhere to in subsequent public appearances. Given that France, Italy and Spain had long urged this kind of reform as a concrete manifestation of solidarity, the Social Democrat Scholz's cautious overture carried great significance as an unequivocally positive signal in terms of the feasibility of a cardinal reform of this nature. When he entered office in the spring of 2018, he mainly represented continuity compared to his predecessor, the Christian Democrat Wolfgang Schäuble. After a few months, however, he joined the growing chorus advocating for some form of common unemployment insurance scheme in the EU, and he announced that he had begun to elaborate on this subject with his French counterpart.

Scholz's declaration revealed a degree of foresight. He knew that crises would continue to occur in the future, and that solidarity would need to be shown when they did. The lack of solidarity at the time of the 2010–14 crisis significantly damaged faith in the EU and led to anti-Brussels forces gaining ground in numerous countries. It was no accident that Pier Carlo Padoan, then Italian finance minister, had in the preceding years been the standard-bearer for common unemployment insurance in ministerial circles.[9]

At the same time, the German political and economic elites – in common with the great majority of public opinion – had long opposed

---

8   Olaf Scholz became finance minister following the September 2017 elections to the Bundestag (and after the failure of the so-called Jamaica coalition), but was no stranger to big politics in Berlin, having held the labour and social affairs portfolio in an earlier grand coalition. He subsequently served as mayor of Hamburg, the country's second most populous city. He became the chancellor of Germany in December 2021.

9   Padoan is a renowned economics professor and former chief economist of the OECD, who also acted as the coordinator of socialist finance ministers in ECOFIN. Once he nailed his colours to the mast, there was a concrete demandeur of this specific policy.

similar solutions that would have led to transfers within the EU, particularly in the eurozone. In reality, Scholz was not even speaking of transfers in 2018, but rather of regressing economies receiving preferential credit in order to improve their provision for the jobless. While there are a variety of possible models for an insurance mechanism, the essence was that at least some initial steps should be taken to ensure that, in the event of fresh financial crises, the eurozone would not head in the direction of economic and social disintegration.

Common European unemployment insurance is not a new idea. As early as the 1970s, when leaders in Brussels thoroughly explored the issue of sustainable monetary union after the unravelling of the first attempt at monetary coordination (the so-called currency snake), they articulated the need for a Union-wide solution to the management of joblessness. The Marjolin Report (1975) unequivocally signalled the need for unemployment insurance (a community unemployment benefit fund), and its message was reinforced by the MacDougall Report on the EU budget (1977). Studies were also prepared during the period of the Maastricht Treaty in the early 1990s, explaining the importance of automatic stabilizers – as in the joint work of Jean Pisani-Ferry and Alexander Italianer (1994). For mainly political reasons, however, this pillar did not become part of the emerging structure – a flaw in the foundations that would be revealed in the crisis of 2010–13.

As the crisis in the EU deepened in 2010–11, many calculations were made that proved that, if such a mechanism had existed, the eurozone would have recovered much more quickly and the social costs of the crisis as a whole would have been far lower. The European Commission called on a number of experts to analyse the situation and outline solutions. One of these experts was Sebastian Dullien, whose book on common provision for joblessness in Europe (Dullien 2014) was later published by the German Bertelsmann Foundation. Dullien conceived of a fund in which every European worker would participate, and from which they would receive immediate support in the event of becoming unemployed, with the option for the worker's own country to supplement or prolong such support.

Dullien's model has been characterized as 'basic common unemployment insurance', which is one of two competing approaches.

The other option is a so-called reinsurance mechanism, also known as a rainy day model. A scheme on the basis of the former approach could be created by a partial pooling of national systems, which would mean receiving unemployment benefits from a common fund for a limited period (e.g. six months) and sharing the costs of that among the member states. Individual workers become part of a risk community. Member states can still top up payments from the common pool and also extend coverage from their own resources as long as they wish, but the very existence of the common pool represents EU solidarity for countries experiencing temporary hardships due to the limitations placed on their macroeconomic toolbox by the monetary union.

Designing a reinsurance scheme would be easier than partial pooling, politically and otherwise. The national fiscal capacity for dealing with cyclical unemployment would be supported, but transfers would only be triggered by major crises. Such a scheme would make a stronger and more visible impact at times of crisis, while lacking a role during more modest fluctuations. The risk of this model lies in setting the trigger too high (in terms of how fast unemployment would need to rise above 'standard' levels) and thus making the mechanism less effective than it could otherwise be.

In a currency union equipped with either model of automatic stabilizers, member states that felt defenceless during the crisis of 2011–13 would be strengthened in their autonomy. Countries that offer others financial assistance would be able to weave a safety net more transparently and within a rules-based system, instead of only making ad hoc interventions carried out with the involvement of non-European actors. Either of the two models would deliver three types of stabilization. Firstly, they would contribute to economic stabilization, by shifting demand and purchasing power to countries and regions that would otherwise need to implement fiscal 'adjustment' and internal devaluation. Secondly, social stabilization would be strengthened as well, by directing the flow of funds towards more vulnerable groups and helping to tame the rise of poverty among the working-age population. The third type is institutional stabilization. EMU is based on rules but the application of these rules has been the subject of academic as well as political debates. While some experts simply recommend ignoring the rules and giving up on them entirely, it is more likely that a modus vivendi could be found through the creation of stabilization tools that would allow the reconciliation of uniform fiscal rules with the need to maintain national welfare safety nets and social investment capacities.

After the European Commission revived the idea of common unemployment insurance in its 'Blueprint' published at the end of 2012 – and kept the topic on the agenda in its 2013 communication on the social dimension of EMU – the issue was also put forward by Italy (as holder of the Council presidency) at informal consultations of employment and finance ministers in 2014. Experts from the Bruegel think tank in Brussels prepared an analysis to kick off the debate. Although ministers – particularly at the session of ECOFIN – were not enthusiastic about the issue, analytical endeavours continued.

Between 2014 and 2016, a consortium under the leadership of the Brussels CEPS institute prepared a series of model calculations, reaching the conclusion that what was needed was the collective reinforcement of the insurance systems of member states (which could be achieved without modifying the Treaty). In this way, while EU-level support would not be a constant presence in provision for the jobless, the EU could step in on a complementary financing basis in the event of more serious crises (using funds accumulated during times of prosperity). Two members of the European Parliament – the German Jakob von Weizsäcker and the Spaniard Jonás Fernández – then brought in experts to draw up a concrete proposal: for member countries experiencing a sudden surge in unemployment, the proposal envisaged support through, in small part, actual transfers and, in larger part, the help of loans.

Jean-Claude Juncker, who assumed leadership of the European Commission at the end of 2014, spoke openly during the 2019 European Parliament election campaign earlier that year – and even prior to the campaign – about new fiscal instruments aimed at stabilizing the eurozone, and he did not rule out sharing the risks inherent in closer cooperation within the monetary union. This could mean a number of things: for example, the pooling of national debts to some extent or the elaboration of automatic stabilizers to share the costs of cyclical joblessness among the member states. As president of the

Commission, however, Juncker did not even come close to presenting a concrete proposal.

One possible explanation for the caution of Juncker and others may be that when fiscal tools of this nature enter the conversation, many immediately start to mention moral hazard and block further discussion. But much depends on the definition of moral hazard. The inherited mechanism most certainly carries such a hazard, since there is really no other way to characterize a situation in which every cost arising from imbalances in the system can be loaded onto weaker-performing ('deficit') countries and poorer groups in society.

The economic rationale for, and necessity of, automatic stabilizers is acknowledged among an ever-widening circle of macroeconomic experts. At the same time, progress in economic and political thinking is indicated in the unequivocal pledge made in 2019 by the new Commission president, Ursula von der Leyen, to introduce unemployment benefit reinsurance, a task that also appeared in the mission letters of two EU commissioners (Paolo Gentiloni and Nicolas Schmit).

Eastern imbalance:
growth without welfare

AT THE EU'S INNER PERIPHERY

For citizens of the new member countries, it was largely the experience of the post-1989 'great transformation' that shaped their key expectations for EU accession: namely, stable and sustainable economic growth leading towards convergence. But based on the experiences of the three decades that followed, it seems clear that after the 'vale of tears' of the 1990s no country reached the long-awaited Canaan promised by EU accession. While in the years preceding the great financial crisis, from 2000 to 2007, most countries in the East-Central Europe region went through a 'reconstruction period', after the crisis the pace of this growth could no longer be replicated.

From the beginning of the 1990s, EU accession became an express desire of societies in the region, and it became a reality for the majority in 2004 (and for Romania and Bulgaria in 2007 and for Croatia in 2013). All this, however, did not lead to the elimination of asymmetries between east and west. Growth in the region has remained strongly dependent on foreign direct investment and – with EU membership – the utilization of transfers from within the Union. National governments were able to take advantage of these opportunities with varying degrees of success, but none were able to pull off a miracle.

Asymmetries between east and west and the underdevelopment of the new member states have led to tensions within the EU. Of course, European integration has never been entirely homogeneous. Prior to the EU's eastward expansion, the original group of six members (integrated in 1957) had already admitted another nine. The 2004 expansion, however, was novel in that the income gap separating the new member countries from the old was far greater than at previous enlargements. For this reason, while capital has largely flowed from west to east, labour has mostly flowed from east to west.

Despite varying paces of convergence in terms of GDP, most countries in the region have so far developed as a kind of inner periphery within the EU. The most important of the aspects that distinguish this periphery from the EU centre is perhaps the dominance in a wide variety of sectors of transnational companies from higher-income OECD countries, but there are also important distinguishing features in the area of labour relations. A gulf is apparent between east and west in the levels of organization of employers and employees, as well as in the strength and prevalence of collective bargaining processes. The latter represents a constant temptation for economic policymakers in the east to strengthen competitiveness to the detriment of workers, while strategies built on vocational training and innovation remain relatively rare.

Coming to terms with the asymmetries within the EU runs into difficulties not only on the eastern side: in Western European countries, too, many find them hard to digest. The EU's eastward expansion meant the accession not only of countries and markets, but also of people – moreover, people with equal rights. Although countries that have welcomed migrant labour are clearly winners from migration in the economic sense, a kind of 'welfare chauvinism' can still be observed among them, turning public opinion against EU migrants. Debates continue to rage within EU institutions on the subject of 'social dumping' (which has led to increasing calls for renewed regulation of the services that reach across the borders of member countries).

In reality, the actual risks related to east–west mobility exist not in the recipient states but in the countries of origin. A significant portion of workers arriving from East-Central Europe are overqualified for the jobs they fill. In 2012, this applied to around half of the migrant workers with a higher education degree. In certain sectors (particularly in healthcare), the emigration of highly qualified people triggers serious tensions.

Compensating somewhat for the risks and losses that come with emigration are financial remittances sent back home (which quickly reached 3% of GDP in the cases of Lithuania and Latvia, and 4% in the case of Bulgaria, in the wake of accession to the EU). However, in the majority of the new member countries, emigration only adds to the existing demographic tension arising from low birth rates. The latter had no small part to play in the fact that Hungary, the three Baltic states, Romania and Bulgaria have all reported continuous population decline over the past decade. This demographic sample is qualitatively different to that of Western Europe, since the longer-established EU member states, besides enjoying higher life expectancies, typically also sustain modest but stable population growth by means of a moderate but continuously positive net immigration surplus.

The eastward expansion of the EU in 2004 and 2007 practically doubled labour mobility within the Union, and the income gap between east and west will remain significant over the long term. Much nevertheless depends on the details, and on the given local economic, social and political situation. For example, although an income gulf exists between the Czech Republic and neighbouring Germany, very few Czechs emigrate permanently. This is obviously partly due to the fact that, despite considerably lower GDP in the Czech Republic, poverty is at a similarly low level to Germany's. A stronger social safety net and the containment of poverty have proven effective brakes on emigration.

Many see the EU as having a centre; namely, the eurozone. For this reason, the introduction of the euro symbolizes a country's arrival at the centre. In reality, however – as discussed in the previous chapter – the eurozone itself can be divided into a centre and a periphery, so that for the countries of the east the immediate prospect is movement from one periphery outside the eurozone to another periphery within it.

Four countries in this region succeeded in introducing the euro in the first decade after EU accession – these were mostly smaller countries (where autonomy in monetary policy carried no great significance in practice, and where little was at stake in surrendering it). In many cases, however, the price of financial success was a sharpening of social inequalities (as in Latvia) or regional inequalities (as in Slovakia). The ability to attain financial convergence (lowering nominal inflation and deficit indicators) can be seen as an achievement of government, but at times of crisis 'internal devaluation' becomes unavoidable. Youth unemployment, poverty and emigration arising in the wake of internal devaluation can undermine the potential for economic growth. Although the long-term sustainability of the model is doubtful, the search for an alternative is, at the same time, the task of the EU as a whole and not just of the impacted countries.

It is no accident that the governments of Poland, the Czech Republic and Hungary – adopting a position contrary to previous governments – are no longer pressing for the euro's introduction, preferring to bide their time. If we look for the main reason for the reluctance of these countries to introduce the euro, it is probably nothing more than a desire to cling on to autonomous decision making. For these countries, accession to the eurozone essentially signifies the choice between even more rules to follow or greater discretionary decision making. Within the current political constellation, in the context of strong Polish, Czech and Hungarian nationalism, the power elites in this group of countries are clearly drawn toward greater discretion and autonomy. For this reason, they accept the risk of being pushed to the periphery within what many see as a two-speed Europe.

In the larger Visegrád countries,[1] the adherence to national currencies is one manifestation of the economic nationalism that has evolved largely as a consequence of the lasting asymmetries brought about by market transition. In the cases of Poland and Hungary, we can speak unequivocally of the hegemony of conservative nationalism, which calls into question numerous enlightenment values (such as the separation of church and state). Although rival ideologies in the forms of liberalism and social democracy remain present, they

---

1   Starting from a regional summit held in the Hungarian town of Visegrád in 1991, the cooperation between Poland, Czechoslovakia and Hungary has seen these countries dubbed the Visegrád Three, and subsequently – following the 'velvet divorce' of the Czech and Slovak Republics – the Visegrád Four. The choice of the venue was a reminder of the summit of Hungarian, Polish and Bohemian kings at the same site in 1335, which helped to overcome Czech–Polish hostilities and paved the way to closer cooperation in security and trade between the three medieval kingdoms.

have lost their opportunity to become the dominant trends as a consequence of the experiences of the transition.

Social democracy became a significant political force in the East-Central Europe region precisely at a time (in the mid-1990s) when the ideology – which represented some of the most important aspirations of the west – had arrived at a junction and became somewhat disoriented. The unexpected trauma of the marketization that followed the collapse of the communist model brought a renaissance of social democracy in East-Central Europe as it underwent systemic change. It may have seemed that social democracy offered a theoretically correct and practically efficacious manifesto for the political left; namely, the implementation of a welfare state along the lines that evolved in Western Europe following World War II. At the same time, the crises of welfare capitalism and the European social model raised existential questions for progressive political tendencies even outside the centre, manifest in the disorientation among centre-left parties.

The nature of the social democratic alternative on the (semi-) periphery is an interesting question in itself. In East-Central Europe – where ideologues of the post-communist political transformation would eventually attempt to dampen the heightened expectations attached to welfare capitalism, citing the differences in the magnitudes of national incomes – the question of alternative models was closely connected to the question of belonging to Europe. The European social model failed to permeate the EU's 'new' member states in the east, both before and after accession; this secured an advantage for conservative and nationalist tendencies, along with their own particular notions about the organization of society.

IN THE PRISON OF THE NEOLIBERAL PARADIGM

From the perspective of welfare policy and social cohesion, the guiding ideas of the political transformation that took place in Eastern Europe – including in the period of EU accession – mostly represented a negative influence. Such concepts and intellectual trends have a major role to play in shaping policy – something that was indeed evident in East-Central Europe following the change of system. But although the expectations of society with respect to that change were focused on convergence with the west, this did not mean that the western-style welfare state would play a central role in the ideologies of the political transformation. Quite the contrary.

The concept of the 'premature welfare state', coined by János Kornai, stands out from the debates of the early transition period (in the early 1990s). By describing failed state socialism in these terms, Kornai – while recognizing the progressive ambitions and partial achievements of social policy – portrayed the countries of the Soviet bloc as attempting to expand social rights beyond their means. In his view, the socialist system had taken on more than it could handle; no 'Swedish' model could be built at the given income levels.

In the 1990s, this essentially economic logic exerted a greater influence on government measures with respect to welfare systems than theories and concepts related to social models. Kornai's concept of the premature welfare state was adopted by the World Bank, helping it gain recognition beyond Hungary. Following Kornai, many accepted that the first consideration when calibrating social provision should be the level of development of the countries in question, and that welfare promises needed to be scaled back. These countries needed to pursue a type of social policy that was proportionate to their 'load-bearing capacity'.

It was possible to arrive at a number of theoretical implications and practical measures from Kornai's thesis, partly with respect to public finances and partly within the private economic sphere. Within the economy itself, one implication was that welfare activities needed to be detached from their incongruous provision by corporations. The state-socialist system had seen levelling or equalizing policies pursued not merely in the context of the welfare state (via transfers) but also through the activities of companies. From the workplace crèche to the summer holiday camp, there were numerous services that would not be listed among the functions of a corporation in an American economics textbook. Over the course of the economic transformation of the 1990s, companies' welfare functions were largely dismantled; moreover, this process held no guarantees that these functions would be systematically taken over by either local governments or the state. This transformation was accomplished partly via privatization and partly through the liquidation of certain state-owned companies and reforms of the public sphere.

Within the social system itself, a paradigm shift occurred as the means-testing principle came to the fore. This principle (in contrast to the universal or insurance-based approach) places people who are truly poor – and measurably and provably so – at the centre of welfare policy. This paradigm shift was personified by economists such as Leszek Balcerowicz in Poland and Lajos Bokros in Hungary (the latter's name is associated with the macroeconomic stabilization programme of 1995 that came to be known as the Bokros package, which coupled measures to restore equilibrium with reforms to speed up change in the welfare model).

Another important area in the 1990s was the opening up of certain elements of the social system to privatization, ushering in the entry of private actors. An example of this was the pension system, where the previous uniform state (pay-as-you-go) system was joined in 1997 by a mandatory private pension pillar. The reform diverted a portion of mandatory pension contributions into a gradually accumulating private pillar, which temporarily resulted in an increase in the public finance deficit. The inspiration for this kind of transformation in the pension system came not from the countries of the EU but from reforms carried out in Chile under the Pinochet dictatorship.

Healthcare reform would have followed a similar template – and it is no accident that around the turn of the millennium Kornai himself also engaged primarily with the economics of healthcare, referring to the sector as the last bastion of the socialist system. The work thinkers such as Kornai were engaged in was aimed at setting the conceptual stage for the privatization of health insurance, or of public–private partnership schemes in healthcare services.

Kornai's concept of the premature welfare state served as received wisdom for the best part of two decades. This contributed to the region's welfare models showing an affinity with the so-called emerging economies, rather than converging towards the rest of Europe. An intellectual kinship could be demonstrated with the more liberal British model, but few understood the significance of that model's central element: a healthcare service that was universal and, in terms of provision, free.

The neoconservative school of thought was applied the most consistently – one might say to its extremes – in Hungary after 2010.

The System of National Cooperation (NER)[2] was declared as a break with the past in numerous areas (constitutionality, economic policy, sports policy, etc.), but in reality it also meant the accelerated scaling back of social rights, taking advantage of the autocratic distortion of the political system. The notion of the welfare state was contrasted with the concept of a 'work-based society'.

If we seek a scholarly foundation for this school of thought in contemporary literature on the subject, we will probably not find it. Writings on the concept of 'workfare' do exist, but these tend to be from the 1980s, and evaluations tend to be negative. Even so, it was in the spirit of this concept that Hungarian Prime Minister Viktor Orbán proclaimed that people must be provided 'work, not benefits'. This signified a change in both the employment and social spheres. Employment policy was reduced in scope. All that was required was to revive the economy by means of a regulatory environment and government support that would be favourable to the SME sector, and to enable employers to employ their workers in the manner best suited to their own needs. Where primary employment offered in this form is insufficient, the organization of community work schemes should help the move towards full employment.

The shortening of the period of entitlement to unemployment benefits to ninety days took place under the aegis of the work-based society, which promoted the dominance of community work in employment policy. Employment and social policy decisions were relegated to a lower level in the administrative hierarchy (with Hungary becoming the sole country in the EU without either a labour or a social affairs minister). Social benefits have become increasingly conditional and have been transferred to become the function of local governments. At the same time, the nature of redistribution has shifted in emphasis, as support increasingly benefits the middle class (for example, the value of child benefits have steadily decreased but family tax benefits have expanded).

---

2   Following the 2010 general elections, which resulted in the right-wing Fidesz party gaining a constitutional majority, this expression was introduced to describe the new system, which was centred around a more nationalistic ideology and autocratic leadership and which lacked adequate checks and balances.

An important series of measures in this period are linked to the pension system, such as the abolition of the mandatory private pillar and the rollback of early retirement. In 2010–11, with a view to consolidating public finances, Orbán – utilizing a combination of coercion and deception – reversed the pension reforms of 1997. At the same time, the maximum state pension was abolished and the gradual increase in the value of the minimum pension was halted, thus opening the way for further precipitous growth in income inequality among the elderly.

Most of the above measures can be regarded, in their own exaggerated and extreme form, as part of a 'typically Hungarian' social policy. Among these, only the effective raising of the retirement age and the related rollback of early retirement conform to an international trend, owing to the general demographic tendencies typical of more advanced countries. Given that the pruning back of the welfare system was the main direction of reform, certain elements of economic regulation were cloaked in social policy when it was politically convenient to do so (e.g. prior to the 2014 elections), with the prime example being the introduction of administrative controls on the prices of key domestic commodities – the so-called utility price cuts.

Although the above is only a partial sketch of all the ideas impacting welfare systems in East-Central Europe, it can clearly be seen that, in a region that is progressively integrating into the EU, the evolution of social policy in the last quarter of a century has been determined largely by doctrines that point towards dismantlement (with fewer resources, a smaller range of state responsibilities and narrower entitlement). While Kornai's premature welfare state and Orbán's work-based society provided the ideological framework for neoliberal reforms, EU accession in 2004 did not in itself prove a development of similar significance.

The role of the European Union in the field of social policy has hardly represented the kind of decisive guiding influence that would permits us to characterize accession in 2004 as the beginning of a new era. While this does not mean that EU accession had no impact at all on social policy in East-Central Europe, the new elements that did emerge (e.g. targeted employment and social programmes) did not give rise to a uniform paradigm with the ability to establish deep roots. Since the eastward enlargement process did not forge a strong attachment to the European social model in the east (Sissenich 2007), the division between paradigms has had long-term consequences. Countries of the East-Central Europe region turned away from building up the welfare state when economic convergence was already happening, and they did not appear particularly receptive to attempts at coordination when the EU called for a strengthening of the social dimension through the Europe 2020 Strategy and the European Pillar of Social Rights.

EASTERN POVERTY: THROUGH A EUROPEAN LENS

The transition to a market economy in East-Central Europe led to considerable social inequality and, at least in the initial years, there were relatively few social policy tools to counterbalance this. The EU exercised only a moderate influence on domestic processes; despite common guidance, each member state was left to find its own way – and so too were the new entrants. While EU membership provided a new framework for the consolidated development of the economy, the notion that what was needed was the operation of a *social* market economy – an idea still important in the 1990s – had become lost to domestic politics.

The switch to a market economy was particularly tragic for the transition countries at the beginning of the process.[3] Gábor Scheiring (2021) estimates that roughly 7.3 million Eastern Europeans lost their lives unnecessarily in this period as a consequence of the deep recession that set in with the shock of capitalism's return and

---

3   The broad category of transition countries, which includes former Soviet republics but also all other countries in East-Central Europe and the Balkans (with the exception of Greece), can be broken down to various subregions based on their economic performance and social outcomes. Unsurprisingly, and as is demonstrated by Ghodsee and Orenstein (2021), the original expectation of a J-curve failed to materialize anywhere, but at least in East-Central Europe a path to prosperity was found from the late 1990s onwards. On the other hand, GDP per capita in 2016 remained below the 1989 levels in Moldova, Georgia, Kosovo, Serbia, Tajikistan and Ukraine. 'For these countries, transition brought unprecedented levels of economic pain and little gain, except for an elite few, for decades' (Ghodsee and Orenstein 2021, p. 9).

the unravelling of existing economic ties and mechanisms. Of especially great significance in this tragic transition was the process of deindustrialization, which saw relatively stable industrial jobs disappear en masse in the first half of the 1990s.

For a region struggling with growing unemployment, poverty and income inequality as a consequence of the transition, it came as a promising development when the EU introduced an increasing number of social initiatives. One important example came in 2010, when the EU specifically elevated the fight against poverty and social exclusion to one of the main goals of its ten-year Europe 2020 Strategy: based on a proposal from the European Commission, leaders of the member countries agreed to lift at least 20 million people out of poverty and social exclusion by 2020.

In EU policy analysis, changes are measured using a set of uniform EU-wide indicators. But measuring poverty is no simple task, as EU officials needed to recognize at the launch of the Strategy. They needed to adopt target numbers for the reduction of poverty that would be able to simultaneously represent both national differences and the pan-European perspective. Union-level targets had to serve as a guide for individual member states, at once clarifying the common European goal and enabling each state – with adjustments to specific national situations and conceptual outlooks – to work towards it.

As a consequence of these considerations, the Europe 2020 Strategy utilizes three poverty indicators. One is financial-statistical, measuring the percentage of the population who live on an income below 60% of the median average in the given country. This is the EU's longest-used index for determining the scale of poverty, and it is similar to that applied by the OECD. Naturally, differences among the member states are extreme in terms of median incomes. This indicator therefore measures whether someone in the given country is poor (in terms of income) compared with the national average. At the EU-wide level, this index stands at around 17–18%, meaning that today more than 80 million people live in poverty within the EU, some 20 million of them children.

However, given that incomes differ between member countries, it is not certain that this indicator in itself gives a true reflection of living situations. For this reason we also use a second poverty indicator: namely, the proportion of low-work-intensity households, meaning households in which there are no residents with a stable working income and where consequently the household is dependent entirely on social support from the state or elsewhere.[4]

There is also a third indicator, which measures severe material deprivation and comprises a total of nine material components.[5] This indicator determines the proportion of the population who are impoverished, as defined by factors such as a lack of basic household items (counting those who are forced for financial reasons to do without at least four of nine specific consumer items). Income alone is of course not the decisive factor in assessing poverty, since much depends on the standard of social services and infrastructure and on the benefits available to families. This is why material deprivation is also an important factor. If we take this as the determining indicator of poverty, then Romania had the highest proportion of poor people in the EU in the post-enlargement decade.

According to data for December 2012 from the EU's statistical office, close to one-quarter of the total population of the EU were threatened with impoverishment in 2011, if we define this as meaning that at least one of the three above indicators applied. When individual member countries had to formulate their own goals and programmes, however, they were able to decide for themselves what weight to assign in their strategies to each factor within a complex indicator. Given that Hungary's government inflated employment numbers in this period by involving several hundred thousand people in community work schemes, where they would be listed among the statistics for the employed, the ratio of households characterized

---

4   To be more precise, this concerns households where individuals aged between 18 and 59 spent less than 20% of their potential working hours in the preceding year actually working.

5   These components are arrears in debt repayments or home bills; the inability to pay unexpected expenses; the lack of a telephone for financial reasons; the lack of a colour TV for financial reasons; the lack of a washing machine for financial reasons; the lack of a car for financial reasons; the inability to take a one-week annual holiday; the lack of meat or protein in one's diet at least every second day; and the inability to adequately heat one's home.

as having 'low work intensity' fell significantly. (In 2016, 8.2% of people in Hungary lived in a household of low work intensity, while this number was as high as 13.6% in 2013.)

Meanwhile, the process of economic development and convergence, combined with recovery from crisis, reduces year by year the number of those classed as suffering severe material deprivation. In Hungary in 2015, 16.2% of the population lived in a household with severe material deprivation, although this proportion was as high as 19.4% a year earlier and was 27.8% in 2013. While a washing machine, television or telephone does not represent a serious expense for the majority, paying off debts still caused serious problems for many Hungarian families even a few years ago, although this is a situation that has changed somewhat in the intervening time.

The Central European region does not present a uniform picture in terms of social mobility. Slovakia, for example, is near the bottom in Europe in this respect, while the Czech Republic is in the middle and Poland is in third place. The three most socially mobile countries in the EU are Cyprus, Greece and Poland. This is not surprising in Poland's case since it has delivered some of the best economic performance in the EU in recent years. Greece's numbers are more perplexing, however, as in the period following the start of the crisis its GDP has shrunk considerably while poverty and social exclusion have greatly increased.

The issue of poverty and how to escape from it is interwoven with the Roma question in several East-Central European countries. Although some older EU member states (such as Spain) also have substantial Gypsy minorities, the Roma question was effectively introduced to the EU through its eastward expansion. Not all Roma are poor, but in Romania, Bulgaria, Hungary, the Czech Republic and Slovakia a gulf continues to separate the Roma minority from the majority of society in terms of education levels, employment, health status and living conditions. Elimination of this gulf – and often even its measurement – is hindered by continually reinforced prejudice, and in many cases by open, politically supported racism.

The precarious social situations that have arisen from the shift in economic philosophies and the upheaval of social policies are becoming unevenly geographically concentrated (via problems such as discrimination against Roma[6]) and increasingly difficult to manage. These trends demand a rethink of the general models of economic and social development, along with the elaboration and implementation of complex developmental and integrative programmes.

HUNGARY GOES TO EXTREMES

In the period since 2010, Hungary has become a focus of international attention as an increasingly autocratic country moving away from democracy and the rule of law. However, at least as important – and indeed closely linked to constitutional concerns – is the fact that under Orbán's rule Hungary has also produced extremes in the social sphere, as the country's system has become ever more distorted. The new Fundamental Law, which replaced the country's constitution in 2011, has gutted social rights. Meaningful social dialogue has been eliminated, while the period of entitlement for unemployment benefits has been reduced to ninety days.

According to Eurostat data, the number of people in Hungary at risk of falling into poverty and threatened by social exclusion in 2016 was 2.54 million, or 26.3% of society. This is a very high proportion, albeit somewhat lower than the 2.79 million measured in 2008. Poverty and social exclusion increased in the ensuing period, right up to 2013, when some 3.4 million people belonged in this category. Eurostat counted 3.1 million poor or excluded people in 2014, and 2.7 million in 2015. The decrease was partly brought about by a pickup in economic growth and a decline in the population. Based on 2015 data, some 23.7% of the EU population as a whole were classed as poor or excluded; the Hungarian figure thus slightly exceeded the EU average.

Although the fall in the number of those threatened by poverty and social exclusion is an important and positive development, a few caveats should be added. On the one hand, it should be noted that indicators of poverty can only show how many people have been added or subtracted from a given category from one year to the next. We cannot discern from that same indicator whether someone who

---

6   Due to this phenomenon, experts have started to speak about rural ghettos in Hungary.

already belonged in the category of the poor or excluded – and has subsequently remained in it – has suffered a further drop in their standard of living, and if so, to what extent. Opportunities to gain a clear picture in this area have only narrowed since the Hungarian Central Statistical Office (KSH) discontinued calculations of subsistence levels. Overall, therefore, the numbers of people at a statistically demonstrable risk of poverty and social exclusion may decrease even if income inequality in a given country is sizeable – or even growing.

For this reason, it is important that we examine social dynamics and conditions based on aspects beyond the EU's synthetic indicator of poverty. This may nuance the picture, while also revealing further anomalies. This is why a Eurofound study entitled 'Social mobility in the EU' is noteworthy. In preparing this study, Dublin-based researchers looked at how likely it was that people in individual EU member states would attain a higher social status, and to what extent they could expect better jobs than their parents had. Hungary featured in last place in this comparison, lagging far behind even the penultimate country on the list, Bulgaria. Moreover, Hungary also placed bottom with respect to both genders, with fewer than 10% of men able to improve their lot, while the ratio for women, though close to double that of men, still remained the worst in the EU.

Beyond indicators of poverty, exclusion and social mobility, data on inequality is also important. On this basis we can see that Hungary belongs among those countries with the greatest growth in income inequality during the crisis (2008–13), as expressed through the Gini index. Contrary to the general pattern, the main reason for this was not the polarization of working incomes but changes in the structure of transfers (i.e. taxes and benefits). While engaging in a verbal battle against neoliberalism, the Orbán government introduced a flat rate for income tax that exacerbated inequalities. In this respect, Hungary sticks out from the crowd; a similar phenomenon was observed only in Sweden (albeit on a smaller scale, and only before the return of the Social Democrats in 2014). At the same time, in the case of Sweden it is clear that the small-scale regressive reform of transfers is not leading to growth in poverty on a similar scale, thanks to a far lesser degree of material deprivation.

One aspect examined by European surveys into material deprivation is whether people have sufficient savings to cover unexpected expenses. At the EU level, one-third of people answer this question in the negative. Among EU member countries, this proportion is the highest in Hungary, at 72%. The lack of household cash reserves represents the kind of financial dependence that – under conditions of restricted democracy – may easily be transformed into political dependence. As Zsuzsa Ferge has continually pointed out, more than a third of Hungarian children are born into poverty. We should not be surprised that a survey conducted in the summer of 2017 revealed that Hungarian citizens view public health and social security as the two most serious problems facing the country.

Taking into account both qualitative and quantitative considerations,[7] 2010 appears to mark the point when Hungary turned away from the European mainstream – not only in its constitution and its culture of governance, but also in terms of social policy. Symptomatic of this was the withholding of wage increases over several years, the shameful diversion of EU funds, the gutting of interest reconciliation, the tearing apart of the social safety net, and the introduction of a bloated, dead-end community work programme. Looking at the numbers clearly demonstrates that Hungary appears to be deviating from the general model, which uses state redistribution in an attempt to compensate for and level-off polarized working incomes and which, except in serious crisis periods, can be pursued with success. As for qualitative features, we have seen above how Hungary's welfare policy is 'enriched' by numerous innovations that do not occur elsewhere.

Some may believe that a willingness to make social 'sacrifices' has served as the foundation for economic success, but unfortunately the facts paints a different picture. In terms of economic growth measured by GDP, the first decade of EU membership did not turn out badly for Hungary; nevertheless, other countries in Central and Eastern Europe performed even better. Overall we can speak of a convergence trend in the region, but while in 2000 Hungary was ahead of Poland, Slovakia, Estonia and Lithuania in terms of GDP per capita, by 2012 these countries had all overtaken it. The loss of this relative position may also explain why scapegoating has

---

7   Systematic analysis of domestic social processes can be found in the biennial *Social Report* series, published by TÁRKI and edited by Tamás Kolosi and István György Tóth.

remained a constant motif in the country's politics, and after the global financial crisis in particular. Existential fears may have played a big part in the anti-migration hysteria that has been stirred up by the populist-nationalist Hungarian government since 2015, which it has persistently exploited to shore up its own political power.

In contrast to the more complex approach typical of Western Europe, from 2015 Hungarian migration policy became one-dimensional. The country's policy could initially be characterized as ill-prepared and muddled, but it later became consciously manipulative. Government rhetoric was often mistaken about the realities on the ground, as with the quixotic struggle against economic migration in the first half of 2015 while an unprecedented wave of political refugees reached Hungary's borders. Giant Hungarian-language posters put up across the country joined the battle against immigrants, and yet the non-Hungarian-speaking refugees arriving at the border would not have been able to read them, even by accident. In the meantime, the government failed to prepare either its own official apparatus or public opinion to manage the refugee issue.

All this inevitably led to an improvised and muddled response to the peak of the migration crisis in September 2015 – a response that also sparked discontent abroad. Serious tensions arose between Hungary and some of its neighbours, while the European Commission initiated an infringement procedure due to significant deviations from the rules pertaining to refugees. The absence of a constructive attitude, combined with general antisocial behaviour, wrecked the country's reputation, paralysing any sensible social debate about cross-border mobility and the real reasons for, and consequences of, migration. The Orbán government – both before and after the failed referendum of 2016 – expended its energy opposing the European majority's conception of refugee policy, and with it the implementation of the decision on the 'relocation' of refugees made by the council of ministers of member countries in September 2015.[8]

---

8   Hungarian refugee policy suddenly changed at the time of the 2022 war in Ukraine, when the government started to use the word 'refugee' instead of 'migrant' and clearly felt no need to replicate its 2015 response by building a fence on the Hungary–Ukraine border. The fact that in previous years the infrastructure of refugee support had been scaled down did little to help when it came to providing quality support to arriving Ukrainians.

Various experts involved in EU policy debates put forward many proposals for the adjustment of the method of distributing refugees based on mandatory quotas (including, for example, that it should take into account the demographic situation in each member country, or enable countries in more difficult situations to set additional conditions). However, the main problem was that resistance was couched in a campaign that did not shy away from xenophobia and religious intolerance, misconstruing the phenomenon of migration and thus damaging the domestic economy and society, as well as foreign relations. The campaign acted as if it were not the case that many thousands of (largely native Hungarian-speaking) migrants had moved to Hungary from neighbouring countries, while guest workers were surreptitiously invited into the country when it became apparent that economic growth was being hindered primarily by very serious labour shortages due to emigration.

SOCIAL DUMPING AND POSTED WORKERS

When attempting to manage the risks related to social problems in the new eastern member countries, EU stakeholders have tended to summarize these issues under the catchword 'social dumping'. Typically, however, the debate around social dumping has focused on the single legislative issue of posted workers. This is one of those things that the average European knows very little about, and yet sharp disputes on the topic continue to rage within EU institutions. At the same time, the debate on posted workers is deeply intertwined with the question of east–west divisions within the EU, many elements of which have featured in the discussions over the last decade and a half.

But how do posted workers differ from those who take on work independently in another EU member country? In this specific form of labour mobility, a worker is taken along (or 'posted') by his or her company to work in another EU member state for a certain period, which may be long or short. When this occurs, a portion of workers in the employ of a company from a given member state are taking up work in another EU member state not independently but as part of an organization, and for a stipulated period. It is important to remember, therefore, that posted workers do not enter the receiving country's labour market independently for as long as they remain employees of a company from the sending member state. The status of these posted workers is regulated by a directive adopted in 1996.

According to European Commission data, the member countries that sent posted workers in the greatest numbers during the period following the EU's eastward expansion were Poland, Germany, France, Luxembourg, Belgium and Portugal. However, the problem had evolved since the period that formed the background to the original regulation of 1996. In practice, the rights of posted workers arriving from the east were in many cases violated by the frequent failure to provide the minimum employment and working conditions to which they were entitled. It seems there were companies eager to fish in these troubled waters, and they were able to do so because of a lack of proper international coordination up to that point. With as many as one-and-a-half to two million posted workers per year at stake, this represented a serious risk. In the decade following expansion, the conflicts only multiplied, as did the protests against abuses, mainly voiced by trade unions in Western and Northern Europe.

For this reason, the European Commission put forward a new directive and related regulation in March 2012, the goal of which was to improve the practical application of the 1996 rules. It did this in order to ensure that the fundamental rights of posted workers, such as the entitlement to wages and holidays, would not be violated in future; that trust in the single market would be strengthened; and that cross-border services in general would be able to operate – and even expand – without undue disruption. As for the details, specific proposals were presented that were aimed at, among other things, promoting cooperation between national authorities in order to facilitate action against intermediary companies that operate irregularly. The Commission's proposal sent the clear message that the rights of employees (including the right to go on strike) are just as important as the freedom to provide services.

The Commission president at the time, José Manuel Barroso, had already undertaken the obligation to improve implementation of the 1996 directive when addressing the European Parliament in 2009. The Spanish EU presidency held a two-day conference on the topic in the spring of 2010 in Oviedo, where the majority of participants agreed that, while the opportunity to post workers can benefit the EU's labour market and the operations of companies, it must not also come with the consequence of neglecting minimal social norms. A year later, in June 2011, the Commission invited all interested parties and experts to another conference at which the keynote speaker was former EU commissioner Mario Monti.[9]

In the spring of 2012, after much analysis and conciliation, the Commission made a proposal for an implementing directive to remedy the situation, aimed at ensuring stricter observance of the rules pertaining to payments, the granting of holidays and social security. As part of this, it placed specific recommendations on the EU negotiating table that would prevent companies from shirking their responsibilities by hiding behind intermediary firms (i.e. subcontractors). Since the single market can only function based on the principle of fair competition, the Commission aimed to tighten controls and ensure conformance to requirements while improving the practical application of existing rules. At the same time – while wishing to avoid undermining the use of this form of employment via stricter regulations, given that it seemed advantageous for the labour market and enterprises alike – it also introduced new instruments to eliminate the possibility that employers might evade the observance of minimal social rights.

Practical guarantees against social dumping and poor working conditions applied particularly to the construction industry, where abuses had occurred most often and in the most diverse forms. The Commission made joint and several liability an EU norm in the construction industry (something that had already been in effect for many years in a number of member states), meaning that companies would be held liable under contracts with subcontracting partners abroad. As for the problem of pay, it was not that the regulations were aimed at directly influencing wage levels for posted workers,

---

9   The former EU commissioner and later Italian prime minister Mario Monti had drawn up an expert document a year earlier that contained a proposal for the direction of the single market's further development, which also highlighted the need to settle the debate over posted workers.

but rather that they intended for workers to be guaranteed the wages to which they were entitled.

The Commission's draft proposal was drawn up after detailed consultations with social partners, taking into account the observations of trade unions and employers, including small and medium-sized enterprises. The proposed measures raised the requirements for informing both employees and companies of their relevant rights and obligations, formulated unequivocal rules on cooperation between national authorities responsible for the posting of workers, and endeavoured to prevent the spread of shell companies[10] that used posted workers to circumvent employment regulations. This last objective was also important in order to stop firms using such dubious techniques to dodge the payment of pension and healthcare contributions.

The 2012 legislative 'posting package' – based on EU case law – included a new regulation whereby the rights of employees (including the freedom to strike) would be treated on an equal footing with the freedom to provide services. However, this was withdrawn by the Commission on witnessing protests from a significant number of member countries. The implementing directive itself, on the other hand, succeeded, and it was duly adopted in the spring of 2014. Even so, the story did not end there, as a group of member states remained dissatisfied, along with some trade unions and socialist parties.

After the formation of the Juncker Commission, the process started again, this time with a targeted review of the 1996 directive and guided by the principle of 'equal pay for equal work in the same workplace'. The stated goal was to ensure equitable wages and a level competitive playing field for posting companies and local companies in the receiving countries, while upholding the principle of the free movement of services. Or to put it another way, the goal was to ensure that no country (or company therein) should gain an undue advantage through posting workers from locations where wages are lower, social dialogue weaker and social insurance more limited.

---

10 Shell companies are those that exist only in name in a given city or country, with the aim of, for example, exploiting regulatory differences when acting as intermediaries on the labour market while simultaneously avoiding observance of the rights of the workers they employ.

The new directive specified that, from the first day of a posting, the same remuneration regulations should apply to posted workers as to local employees in the receiving member state, and furthermore it clarified the previously ambiguous rules on benefits. The concept of long-term posting was also introduced, whereby an employee can be posted for an extended period and then, after twelve months have elapsed (following a maximum six-month extension), the posted worker will be subject to the labour laws of the receiving country in almost every respect. It was also prescribed that labour agencies should guarantee the same conditions to posted workers as they do to casual workers employed in the member state where the work is to be carried out.

Thanks to the revised Posting of Workers Directive of 2018, cooperation has intensified among member countries with respect to countering fraud and abuse committed in connection with posted workers, while the number of potential collective agreements has also risen. The deadline for incorporating the directive into law in the member states and the starting date for its application was two years from the date the directive came into effect. In the case of the international road transportation sector, however, it was decided that the provisions of the directive should apply from the day that the planned future sector-specific regulations enter into effect.

COMPETITIVENESS MISCONSTRUED

With the aim of accelerating economic convergence, tools such as low taxes and low wages have become defining elements of the East-Central European model. Proponents of this paradigm see restrained wages as the main source of competitiveness, while viewing the welfare state as a danger to economic development. In their eyes, the occasional slight upward momentum in wage increases is a cause not for satisfaction but for alarm. This conceals the attitude that, from a global perspective, such economies belong to the category of 'small, open and export-oriented' – with everything else that implies. Although the economic policies of the new EU member countries aspired to competitiveness, those who devised them had a lot of catching up to do in their understanding. Every element of their strategies had serious drawbacks. To name two of the most obvious missteps: corporate taxes were significantly reduced; and wages were held at low levels, assisted by a brake on minimum wage increases and by a weakening of representation for employee interests.

As things in the region stand today, it should principally be acknowledged that a unilateral overdose of subsidies aimed at aiding competitiveness is producing negative counter-effects. The low real value of wages is leading to significant emigration, with the effect of draining certain professions of their lifeblood; in general, the workforce increasingly appears as a narrowing cross-section of what should be a wide pool of skills, which hinders companies' growth. However, the problem is bigger and more complex than this. Firms may be quick to welcome measures to boost their competitiveness, but if artificial support on this scale enters the system, then they may easily become complacent and think even less about innovation, technical modernization, and research and development. R&D expenditures in proportion to GDP fell far behind the desired target of 3% in the East-Central Europe region in the period of EU accession (typically hovering at about 1% of GDP), before beginning to rise thereafter. At the same time, even with a growth (or subsequent stagnation) in R&D expenditures, the number of research jobs has dwindled considerably, as has the number of people actually working in research and development – which, again, is rather bad news.

For this reason it comes as no surprise that, while at first glance the East-Central Europe region does all it can for competitiveness, organizations that regularly assess this metric do not issue favourable reports. Among these is the World Economic Forum (WEF), on whose international league table Hungary has slipped progressively lower in pursuit of cost-competitiveness. A wrong course cannot be corrected too quickly, however. While economic policy, with a view to greater future growth, can impact every component of the synthetic WEF index, each country's level of competitiveness changes only slowly with time – or, more precisely, only slowly improves. This is even truer of factors such as the unpredictability of the institutional environment or the weakening of the rule of law (the main causes of Hungary's declining reputation).

Trust in institutions is easy to lose but difficult to rebuild (just as it proved very difficult, despite improving macroeconomic indicators, for Hungary to climb out of the 'junk' category not recommended for investment). Unfortunately, Hungary's small-statism did not create an 'entrepreneurial state' in the sense that Mariana Mazzucato – or any other serious economist – would evaluate favourably, and so its positive impact is visible neither on the WEF table nor in reality. Reacting to these concerns, the Hungarian government set up a Competitiveness Council.[11] In a system that assumes more and more autocratic features with each passing week, any functioning council or interest conciliation forum would be welcome; however, it is worth mentioning that when a similarly named body was formed under the previous (socialist-liberal) government, it also included workers' representatives.

Interestingly, during the 2016–17 period – when the EU as a whole could no longer be described as being in crisis– a renewed diagnosis of deteriorating competitiveness coincided with another grave problem: the emergence of growing labour shortages. This in turn impacted the former problem: for the first time, wage convergence – rather than wage restraints – appeared among the criteria of competitiveness. This would be insufficiently newsworthy if it were only workers' representatives within the region who were talking about it; however, pronouncements in this spirit also issued from institutions such as the OECD and the European Bank for Reconstruction and Development (EBRD). The explanation for this widespread attention is that, even in a small, open economy, wages cannot be regarded merely as a cost factor. Viewed in the aggregate, wages are at once a factor of demand at the macroeconomic level and a source of livelihood for workers (and their families). Moreover, wages not only cover consumption, but are an investment in human capital, the very source of growth. Whoever fails to take this into account may find their competitive advantage to be only temporary.

In reality, competitiveness (and thus economic growth potential) is also weakened by the counterproductive migration policies witnessed across a large part of the region. The labour market is

---

11   In this period the European Commission had also urged the formation of competitiveness councils.

a dynamic system not only within individual national economies but also between countries. Properly regulated immigration may signify a major competitive advantage in terms of growth potential for receiving countries. And, conversely, countries that fail to build a labour import infrastructure (including tools supporting integration into the labour market and the school system) may suffer a considerable competitive disadvantage. Bogus rhetoric about halting migration helps neither society nor economic actors find their way to success amid the complex maze of economic competition. Migration policy in East-Central Europe thus needs reviewing, for reasons of economics, demographics and human resources management alike.

For the recently integrated EU member countries, the problems faced by sectors characterized by high unemployment and inactivity are primarily caused not by technological factors (robotization, digitalization, etc.), but by developmental failures and omissions. Hungary is often a prisoner of extremes in this regard as well. For example, the structural changes that have been taking place in the school system do little to help confront the challenges of the new technological revolution. The lowering of the school leaving age, the acceptance of trends towards segregation, and the stagnation (or decline) in the teaching of foreign languages all potentially put Hungary in an increasingly disadvantaged position in international economic competition. All these trends may also become entrenched as persistent dangers for social cohesion. In the spirit of the Europe 2020 Strategy, Hungary set itself the ambitious goal of raising the employment rate to 75% (among those aged 20–64). In the period following the major crisis of 2008–9, however, community work schemes became the dominant tool of state employment policy – without offering any chance for those employed in such schemes to graduate to quality jobs on the primary labour market.

In 2021, with the support of the Friedrich Ebert Foundation, the Vienna Institute for International Economic Studies (WIIW) completed a study examining how East-Central Europe might leave behind all the distortions and blind alleys that the change of political system had forced the region to haphazardly develop, often through decisions undertaken in conditions of severe pressure and uncertainty. The study urged a new growth model,[12] with national innovation systems as its essential elements, and with a leading role to be taken by the entrepreneurial state in the sense suggested by Mazzucato.

A re-examination of the region's progress down these developmental dead-ends – which are connected to the slowdown in growth and to the emerging labour shortages – has thus begun, and it becomes even more timely in light of new ideas around the future of work. One of the main pillars of sustainability is quality vocational training (acquiring 'horizontal' skills in the school system) coupled with the development of, and wider access to, institutions of lifelong learning. A turnaround in wage policy should thus be embedded in a more general paradigm shift in economic and human resources policy. Such a reorientation would also need to address the duality of excessively low and excessively high incomes.

Generally speaking, boosting economic growth potential requires governments in the East-Central Europe region to re-evaluate the role of human resources in growth, attaching greater weight than before to investment in human capital. In the fields of public education, national health and social integration – hitherto characterized by the withdrawal of funding – new investments are needed to ensure that the second decade of EU membership brings tangible improvements for society. The EU allocated plentiful funds for the achievement of these goals in the budgetary period up to 2020. The European Social Fund could provide substantially more help in advancing employment for women, helping young people start careers, integrating Roma, improving integration of the disabled into the labour market and promoting active ageing. What is also required is political will at the local level and the ability to manage the available resources fairly.

---

12   Marcin Piatkowski (2018) similarly pushed for a new growth model, despite regarding the region's growth as impressive and presenting Poland's performance within it as a kind of economic miracle. In his conception, the Washington Consensus needs to be replaced by a Warsaw Consensus.

A digital future: fears and dreams

THE FEAR OF ROBOTS AND THE TRANSFORMATION OF LABOUR

The past decade has seen the emergence of a spate of analysis – and, let us admit, conjecture – that examines the extent to which our lives are being transformed by the advent of the latest technological era of digitalization, automation and robotization, and by the so-called fourth industrial revolution (or 'Industry 4.0') unfolding in the wake of these technologies. Computerization has brought about changes in the organization of the economy and the evolution of labour, and techno-optimism has been replaced by anxiety over whether these consequences may actually represent an existential threat for many.

Around the turn of the millennium – when broadband internet networks were still being built up, and as desktop computers gave way to laptops and then smartphones – technological advances (specifically around digitalization and the resultant innovations in information and communications technology (ICT)) tended to awaken positive sentiments and expectations. This applied to the impact of the new technologies on economic performance, quality of life and job opportunities alike. The feeling that 'this is the way the world is going' became palpable, as did the expectation that the number of digital jobs would grow, and hence so would the demand for a workforce with an understanding of ICT.

In time, however, euphoria has given way to panic. An increasing number of people take the view that we do not just stand on the threshold of epochal change, but that we already have one foot over it (though expectations today often point in conflicting directions). Though it may not be the end of the world, a sense of 'the end of work' has nevertheless taken hold: the fear of what will happen to us 'if the robots come'. But how many jobs will computers actually take away from us? Who will end up unemployed, and for whom will this be a long-term issue rather than a temporary one? Because if the predictions prove true and within a few decades there are only half as many jobs as there are now, then it is certainly true that dramatic change is on the way.[13]

We find numerous examples of the social impacts of digitalization and automation in everyday life. Day after day we meet people whose jobs will soon disappear as a consequence of technological change. In certain major cities we may still encounter ticket inspectors when using public transport, but in most places this unskilled work has long since been displaced by ticket machines. Even where it has not, it is probably only a matter of time before the introduction of the kind of electronic ticketing system that has become a natural component of mass transit networks across many of the world's major cities (including in Europe).

This is just a single example, familiar to all, of how technology is supplanting human labour under the guise of the modernization of the economy. It remains open to debate, however, whether we fall into the trap of losing a sense of proportion when we project what we find to be true about certain professions or sectors onto the economy as a whole. This is a long-favoured topic in economics. It is not unusual for politicians to shift the blame for joblessness and low incomes onto autonomous changes in technology, but in reality the phenomenon known as 'technological unemployment' remains largely misunderstood.

The focus in the specialized literature – and in broader society – on the digital (previously 'microelectronics') revolution as a 'megatrend' did not emerge only in the last few years, and neither did the assessment of its sociological and economic impacts. Since the 1970s, social researchers have intensively followed the many technological changes that, in the wake of mass computerization, have led on the

---

13   A pair of Oxford academics, Carl Benedikt Frey and Michael Osborne, played a major role in the outbreak of this 'fear of robots', predicting in a paper published in 2013 that 47% of American jobs would become susceptible to computerization. This prediction has increasingly cropped up in the widest range of articles and dissertations ever since.

one hand to a kind of revolution in productivity and on the other to the periodic fear of large-scale job losses. This fear has only been exacerbated by the erosion of industrial jobs in developed countries, brought about by shifts in the international division of labour as a result of globalization.

Today's 'fear of robots' thus resembles the similar fear that swept through labour markets around the turn of the millennium: that many millions of jobs might simply migrate to China. Since then it has turned out that manufacturing jobs in developed countries may migrate not only to China but also to Indonesia, Vietnam and beyond. The two waves of job migration – from domestic to global labour markets, and from human to robot workers – are similar in that they each represent a major transformation that also endangers the balance of employment in Europe. The difference between them is that, while the new international division of labour in the era of globalization has so far tended to draw away industrial jobs requiring mid-level qualifications, the cross hairs are now fixed on low-skilled service and auxiliary jobs. At the same time, artificial intelligence is also knocking at the door, meaning the robots may displace activities and professions that are more complex and creative.

One point that can be made about both these waves is that the more developed countries would do well to respond to the challenges by investing in human capital. The adaptation of education and training is one important area where governments need to react to technological change. Countries in Europe that are pursuing this path (e.g. the Netherlands and Sweden) are at the vanguard of tech-nological innovation while still managing to maintain high levels of employment and social cohesion. If we look outside Europe, the example of Japan should give pause for thought to those who see the proliferation of robots as an obstacle to full employment.

As Aaron Benanav (2020) points out, the proportion of those employed in the manufacturing industry in countries at the fore-front of robotization (such as Germany, Sweden and South Korea) is higher than the average for developed countries. The explanation for this apparent paradox is that robotization helps large industrial companies preserve their competitiveness, with a consequently greater chance of salvaging industrial jobs than companies that, for one reason or another, have fallen behind in the introduction of new technologies.

A third major trend presenting a common challenge in Japan and Europe alike is demographic change – or more precisely the ageing of society. In Europe the era is already upon us when, year after year, the number of people exiting the labour market through retirement exceeds the number entering it. Immigration from outside Europe alleviates this trend only to a very small extent, while internal migration within the continent exacerbates it in many countries (mainly on the EU's eastern periphery). When seeking responses to the advent of the new technological era, we must therefore remain mindful of these parallel trends.

BIG DATA BUSINESS MODELS

The 1990s brought the rapid spread of the internet. Where they could, states supported the roll-out of broadband internet capacities through substantial investment, providing a kind of 'information superhighway' for commerce, which was thus able to enter new dimensions in the virtual world. All this investment created the capacity to gather, process and utilize vast quantities of data, and with the help of the new technology all of this could take place rapidly, at scale and with calculable results. At the same time, it became increasingly clear that the benefits of this capacity could easily become concentrated among certain commercial or political actors: that without adequate regulation these new tools might serve not society as a whole but the interests of the owners of the data-processing mechanisms as well as other powerful groups.

Whether technology overall is a blessing or a curse for human society is a question that runs through the past 200 years of social science. The same question has been at the centre of the almost-continuous research into the social impacts of computerization, robotization and the microelectronics revolution. Among its many other areas of interest, the Club of Rome started examining in the 1970s and 1980s (i.e. before the appearance of the internet) the impact of microelectronics on the rapid spread of computers (see Friedrichs and Schaff 1982).

What early researchers could not yet have discerned was the effect technology would have on enterprises and market structures. And yet it seems today that this is the missing analytical link needed to understand the connection between the dawn of the new technological era and the evolution of income distributions. In his book *The Profit Paradox* (2021), Jan Eeckhout demonstrates that, while new technologies have brought tremendous advantages with respect to living standards across society, they have also resulted in the rise of new, dominant corporations. In this competition, the winner takes all – courtesy of the combined effects of intra-company innovation and weak competition policy. The successes of these dominant companies, as reflected in their huge profits and runaway share prices, do not translate into benefits for their workers: hence the idea of a 'profit paradox'. In Eeckhout's view, this market power needs to be restrained, as it was in the early twentieth century when the first wave of antitrust policies put paid to the era of the robber barons.

Based on fresh scholarly research, personal experience and telling examples, Eeckhout reveals how the market power of companies, across very diverse sectors (from brewing to textiles to advertising), becomes detrimental to workers. He also demonstrates how market power exacerbates other social problems, such as climate change, increasing mortality for certain groups, and a lack of social and geographic mobility. This may simply be because bigger companies have greater financial means at their disposal to persuade politicians not to take action (or to make decisions that expressly promote a continuation of harmful activity).

For their part, the big digital companies do not leave the task of lobbying to others. The growth of the digital industry is illustrated by the fact that the top companies in the sector spend approximately €100 million per year on lobbying EU institutions – or, in other words, on attempting to influence the processes and outcomes of deliberations on EU-wide regulation. This amount far exceeds what traditional industries devote to similar goals. It is worth bearing this in mind when we speculate on why any action to counter the distorting impact on competition of a major technology firm's activities requires five to six years of preparation, or potentially even longer.

The revolution in ICT has triggered a particularly rapid transformation in the media sphere, placing the users themselves in the service of commercial interests – the very same readers, listeners and viewers whom the media was originally meant to serve. A press sustained by advertising revenues is by no means a new development: it has been around for the best part of two centuries. However, this is the first time in history that a mass readership (in the form of today's internet users) has taken on the character of a simple commodity. Without our knowledge or consent, 'profiles' compiled from our personal data are now sold for hundreds of billions of dollars to companies wishing to advertise themselves in every corner of the world.

In this case, the invisible hand of the market is able to employ evermore obscure algorithms in the interest of increasing their potential returns on capital. Moreover, the algorithms that are reshaping the world at such a rapid pace truly are invisible. Everyone experiences on a daily basis how online ads are becoming more and more intrusive, purposefully targeting potential new customers. The strategic military application of technology is even more concerning. Traditional notions of international law are of no use in the age of digital warfare, since they say nothing about acts of internet aggression.

At the same time, new technology is serving to restructure not only the relationships between companies and consumers but also labour relations within companies themselves. According to Shoshana Zuboff, the ICT revolution has led to the evolution of 'surveillance capitalism', of which the new surplus input and source of profit is accessible data on consumers and employees alike. In the absence of adequate supervision and regulation, all of this results in an untraceable and uncontrolled erosion of individual autonomy. As these powers of surveillance reach new levels, the consequences are extremely disquieting not only for the economy but also for the political sphere.

One important risk factor associated with the information economy is the circulation of (and trade in) personal data, potentially violating the rights of individuals to control data about themselves. This risk affects all societies exposed to expanding information systems, but it was in Europe where the protection of personal data was first prioritized and secured, through EU legislation known as the

GDPR.[14] Following the introduction of legislation on data protection, the EU also endeavoured to pioneer the forceful regulation of artificial intelligence (AI). In April 2021 the European Commission unveiled a long-awaited proposal to regulate AI, which represented the first initiative of its kind globally. The bill identified high-risk applications of AI, such as the monitoring and evaluation of a worker's behaviour and performance, or controlling the time a worker spends in front of the computer when teleworking. The goal of this European regulatory effort was no less than to set a world standard for human-centric, trustworthy AI, and to ensure that new technologies develop without undermining social rights.[15]

Beyond the threats automation poses to employment and the dangers of the exploitation of data, greater attention has recently been paid to the quality of the jobs that employ these new technologies. An increasing number of studies attempt to gauge the risks that both companies and employees are inclined to ignore, despite their potentially painful and costly consequences. Such risks include, for example, the links between computerization or mobile telephony and musculoskeletal disorders or other trauma (arising from repetitive work that puts strain on the spine, metacarpus and eyes), the impact of mobile technology and flexible working times on relaxation and sleeping habits (and how this relates to productivity), and

---

14 The General Data Protection Regulation (GDPR), which entered force in 2018, is the toughest privacy and information security law in the world. It was drafted and passed by the EU, but it imposes obligations on organizations anywhere in the world as long as they target or collect data related to people in the EU. If you process the personal data of EU citizens or residents, or you offer them goods or services, then the GDPR applies to you even if you are not an EU citizen or do not reside in Europe. The GDPR imposes fines against those who violate the European privacy and security standards (with penalties reaching tens of millions of euros).

15 Italian member of the European Parliament Brando Benifei, who as rapporteur was responsible for EU legislation on AI, has been pushing for restricting the use of facial recognition technology by law enforcement, with the exception of using it to fight serious crime. He also wants to see civil society and social partners more involved in the regulatory process, especially as regards the use of AI in the workplace.

the socialization of the new generation growing up in the ICT bubble.[16] More research into these risks is needed in order to facilitate government responses that would mitigate them effectively.

ADAPTATION STRATEGIES

The successive waves of the technological revolution represented challenges to the established order in both the economy and society alike. The present experience with digitalization and robotization, coupled with breakthroughs in AI, can be viewed in these terms. International organizations – as well as those within the EU framework – are continuously taking stock of the nature, speed and consequences of these changes. 'Adaptation' is an important notion both for individuals and for economic and political actors; at the same time, there is an unequivocal social requirement to maintain supervision over technological changes, as well as to reconcile the potential of technology with the need to sustain quality employment and social cohesion.

The robot debate has compelled major international organizations to take a stance, among them the OECD, which – in a major study examining the situation in twenty-one countries – put the proportion of jobs that are automatable at 9%, thereby taking a far more sober and cautious attitude to the challenges and dangers ahead than most previous predictions. A few simple examples suffice to clearly illustrate why we can breathe easily when it comes to the proliferation of digital tools and automation. If we take the example of GPS navigation devices assisting drivers, we can see that these have not replaced the drivers themselves but only maps in printed paper form, just as autopilots in aviation did not make living, breathing human pilots redundant. For another, similar example, sensors that scan the prices of products were patented back in the 1950s, and yet the retail

---

16 In theory, young people have an advantage in their ability to master the new technologies, and to thereby achieve more rapid economic success. However, warning signs remain in the shape of drastic changes in reading habits, the abandonment of collective advocacy and the potential vulnerabilities related to mobility – all of which may mean in the longer term that certain advantages of today's younger generation will prove only temporary.

sector has remained a very important employer. Of course, the past is the past, and we cannot necessarily predict the future based on earlier examples. Nevertheless, in most instances even today, machines do not take over entire jobs but only certain actions within them.

Though moderate in its estimate of job losses, the OECD's analysis also reveals that, beyond simply leading to the disappearance of a modest portion of jobs, the digital revolution is thoroughly reshaping a further one-quarter of the labour market, with the remainder also affected in some way. These research findings provided input for the OECD's new Jobs Strategy adopted in 2018. Both the OECD and the International Labour Organization stress that automation does not simply happen: it is a process that can be guided and regulated. If it saves companies and employers money, they will replace human labour with machines; however, the speed and conditions of this process can be influenced by state regulation, and by dialogue and consultation with those affected.

At the time of the major world economic crisis of 2008–9, the digital transformation represented a breakout point for the developed countries of Europe, where governments increased their efforts to hitch onto the momentum that private investment had been directing. In 2010, the EU launched its Europe 2020 economic and social development strategy, announcing 'smart, sustainable and inclusive growth' as its goal. One flagship initiative of the strategy was its digital agenda, under which the European Grand Coalition for Digital Jobs was launched in 2013 on the assumption that an increase in jobs could, and should, be envisaged in this area. Simultaneously, the European Commission launched the Startup Europe programme to assist internet enterprises. In addition to the goal of exchanging knowledge and experience, cooperation of this kind is aimed at ensuring that interested parties can exercise greater influence on the formation of EU policy and the mobilization of resources.

In June 2016, the European Commission published an analysis on the 'future of work', with a focus on developing expertise and skills. There is nothing surprising in this: the EU's response conforms to a two-decade-long trend aimed at developing human capital and labour competitiveness with a view to achieving a high level of employment; and, with this goal in mind, the EU has long been urging increased participation in higher education in member countries as well as the progressive reform of vocational training. The aim of promoting the technological transformation is therefore closely intertwined with the upcoming tasks of education, training and investment in human capital.

In the past two decades in the EU member countries – thanks in part to common long-term development strategies – the number of those participating in higher education has grown significantly while the proportion of the workforce with only a basic education has fallen. Progress has also been made in reducing the rate of early school leaving. However, growth in the number of students in higher education does not in itself provide a satisfactory solution if the content of that education does not change in the meantime; efforts should also be made to ensure that schoolchildren, too, acquire as many 'horizontal skills' as possible (such as emotional intelligence, leadership and communication).

The advent of the new technological era nevertheless calls into question not only the sustainability of employment levels, but also the future of previously evolved social models. For this reason, EU institutions are also intensively occupied with the issue of how modes of labour organization and employment,[17] altered in the wake of the digital revolution, are impacting social rights – and above all social security. In its report of December 2016 relating to the so-called Social Pillar, the European Parliament called on the European Commission to harmonize the new forms of employment with established European models of social security and welfare, and to submit draft legislation accordingly.

Although the United Kingdom was already on its way out of the EU during this period, its government embarked on a similar course to EU policy in this area. The then British Conservative Prime Minister Theresa May asked the political strategist Matthew Taylor to elaborate a comprehensive programme for renewed regulation of working practices. The goal was to retain the flexibility facilitated by technology while filtering out the problematic elements that could

---

17   Such modes encompass those employed under zero-hour contracts or working on various online platforms, such as the alternative taxi companies expelled from Hungary but operating successfully elsewhere.

represent a threat to progress in working conditions and wages. The intention here was not to push back on the so-called gig economy but to ensure proper protection for those working within it. This thorough review of modern working practices, and the measures it generated in 2017 (one year after the referendum triggering Britain's exit from the EU), were targeted at building a better, more equitable labour market, and indeed a better, more equitable country.

The International Labour Organization (ILO), which marked the centenary of its foundation in 2019, has offered a kind of synthesis of the research into the future of work, overseeing a discourse over several years on the changing world of work and the consequences of the latest technological paradigm shift. By its nature, the ILO primarily examines the issue from the perspective of furthering social justice, looking at its impact on inequality and working conditions. Another key aspect for both the EU and the ILO is the way in which working conditions evolve alongside the latest technological changes, particularly in the context of flexible forms of employment, reconciling work and private life, and advances in labour safety.

The ILO describes its approach as human-centred, since it aims to increase investment in people's capabilities, in the institutions of work and in decent and sustainable jobs. The ILO's Centenary Declaration of 2019 calls on member countries to ensure that all their citizens benefit from the changing world of work, as well as ensuring the continued relevance of the formal employment relationship and adequate protection for all workers. It also emphasizes the importance of inclusive and sustainable economic growth, full employment and decent working conditions. Since the ILO obviously has no substantive executive mechanism with respect to member countries, the principles and objectives contained in the declaration serve more as a guide for its own future operation.

EQUAL FOR ALL? THE DEBATE OVER BASIC INCOME

Many believe that the impact of job losses arising from the advent of the new technological era can be managed and softened through fundamental social reform, and more specifically through the introduction of an unconditional basic income (UBI) for citizens. UBI has been – and continues to be – a topic of much debate, but so far it has made only limited inroads into government spheres. For many, the issue of robotization has now invested the debate with new relevancy. Proponents of UBI trace the idea all the way back to Thomas Paine, the romantic thinker of the eighteenth-century French and American revolutions. Such ideas follow almost in a straight line from the Enlightenment ideals of reason and egalitarianism,[18] assuming a requisite injection of radicalism, of course.

Whatever its origins might be, UBI is a prominent topic of debate in our unsettled world and it will remain so for some time to come. It is a radical idea, though not in the sense of being aimed at fundamentally altering the economic or political order. In reality, proponents of UBI accept the existing economic system and its dominant trends as more or less a given, but they recommend radical changes in social policy. For a long time, the basic philosophy behind welfare policy has been that, amid economic conditions that generate inequalities, it should provide support to those who are weaker or are lagging behind. While the market mechanism polarizes, state redistribution levels the playing field. Yet, for some reason, many now see it as better for social policy to offer equal benefits to all. Why is this? Traditional welfare states have weakened or fallen into crisis, say the proponents of UBI. Neither full employment nor income stability can today be regarded as guaranteed (as a consequence of globalization and financial crises, among other reasons). Recent decades have also seen the robot revolution emerge as a new factor, raising the prospect of the accelerated erosion of jobs and social security. A new kind of safety net is therefore required.

Against this backdrop, it is interesting that an online petition was launched in 2020 in a bid to have the European Commission examine – and the European Parliament debate – the possible introduction of a basic income. This would have required the collection of at least a million signatures from at least seven EU countries, with varying quotas from each country (including 16,500 signatures from Hungary, for example). However, the drive failed to gather the requisite number of signatures, so the matter was not pursued at the EU level. Even so, it

---

18   In one of his most famous poems, the nineteenth-century Hungarian poet Sándor Petőfi imagined a time 'when all men lift the horn of plenty in one happy equality'.

did end up being pursued within some individual countries, with one notable example being Finland, where the centre-right government in power at the time conducted a basic income experiment.

Nevertheless, the essence of the Finnish UBI concept was not new benefits but simplification of the existing system. Rather than introducing an additional item of expenditure, the Finns aimed to cancel many existing items in parallel with the introduction of UBI (which, in this trial phase, was only for a group of selected individuals living across various locations). The plan was that, if the experiment proved a success, the system of social benefits would be simplified. Finland's experiment had the potential to inspire other countries: on the one hand because it concerns a rich country, and on the other because the experiment was conducted by a right-wing government, while previously UBI has tended to be discussed more in left-wing circles. But even though no negative effect on employment was observed following the experiment, it has had little international influence. Besides, when the Social Democrats returned to power after the scheme concluded, they did not direct any significant political or financial resources towards similar schemes.

Simplification is almost always an attractive notion, especially in public finances. The existence of a basic income could be seen as obviating the need for the benefits (unemployment or otherwise) that currently allow people a sufficient income for their survival – benefits that are subject to the measurement of their necessity and that are provided only under strict conditions and in ways that may be stigmatizing for the recipients. But wherever means testing is applied, including in the potential case of UBI, it tends to entail differentiated provision. One very significant Hungarian study of UBI models (by István Bánfalvi's working group) made a proposal for provision not to be a uniform amount but to be differentiated according to life situation.[19]

---

19 Besides the publication and ensuing discussion of Bánfalvi's subsistence-money concept (proposing that children receive 25,000, adults 50,000 and expectant mothers 75,000 forints of so-called subsistence money monthly from the state, under the simple 'right to subsist'), the Hungarian edition of *Basic Income* (2014), by Yannick Vanderborght and Philippe Van Parijs, helped deepen debate on the topic in Hungary.

A few problems nevertheless remain. As far as unemployment benefits are concerned, the amount is generally determined in some proportion to lost income. Their replacement by a uniform benefit would therefore seem unfair (and many already regard it as unfair if uniform income support is only granted after 12–18 months). If, on the other hand, the basic income received by the unemployed is adjusted with supplementary unemployment benefits, then rather than simplifying things we have introduced an additional complication to the system. Of course, these may seem like technical details; after all, in the case of UBI the political message is more important. For those espousing the notion of a basic income, this is precisely one of the key arguments: that UBI would guarantee the right to live with dignity, a right declared in the Charter of Fundamental Rights of the European Union. Participants and chroniclers of basic income experiments also argue convincingly that, far from destroying recipients' work ethic, guaranteed income stability for the poor enhances working capabilities, not to mention improving conditions for raising children.

Even so, if we consider all the different situations with which modern social policy must grapple, even more unanswered questions still confront us. For example, how helpful is it for homeless people to receive a basic income determined at a low level? Naturally, for a homeless person to live properly as opposed to merely surviving, they would need a level of support considerably greater than the basic amount – albeit only for a short time in the ideal scenario. Additionally, how can such a reform promote the long-term employability of minorities living in disadvantaged regions? Would it not relieve the government of other important duties if policymakers were to regard social care as settled via the provision of basic income? And – moving from the social questions to the theoretical – why is it that many regard the concept of basic income as belonging more to the neoliberal mindset, linked to the name of Milton Friedman?

Many would probably agree that in times of crisis and growing inequality we should try to extend greater assistance to those on lower incomes. But how can we justify providing some kind of benefits not only to those in need but to everyone, including the highly educated and those with significant wealth – and, moreover, providing it to the same extent? Can the vision of automation really not embrace a continuing commitment to high levels of employment and the institutional system that helps achieve this, recognizing the integrative role of work in society?

These few questions are sufficient to illustrate that solutions to the complexities of UBI are far from self-evident. Conditionality has been the main trend in social policy over the past 10–15 years. Further, there has been declining interest in UBI, even among proponents of universal solutions. One reason for this decline might be that, in recent years, concepts such as universal basic services and job guarantees have received increasing attention, resulting in a kind of rivalry. A still far more powerful principle than the idea of a uniform benefit might be for society as a whole to form a community of risk to support those affected by emergencies (problems with housing, serious illness, etc.) to the extent that the given situation demands. At best, the consensus today extends as far as accepting that, alongside a minimum wage, there is also the need for a minimum income, and that economic policy must strive for both society-wide income security and an inclusive labour market.

COMPETITION, INNOVATION AND THE ENTREPRENEURIAL STATE

Because of the complexities surrounding UBI, many might say that the clearest path to greater prosperity is offered by incentivizing growth and competitiveness rather than by expanding redistribution. This may well be so, but can we state unequivocally where these possibilities would emerge amid the technological transformations and global economic conditions of today? The notions of both growth and competitiveness have been called into question in recent decades as a consequence of world economic trends, uneven development and – last but not least – the ecological crisis. The need for economic growth is not self-evident, particularly if it means nothing more than increasing GDP. The situation is no easier with regard to the concept of competitiveness, whose most vehement critic in international scholarship, the Nobel laureate Paul Krugman, sharply condemns the notion that the competitiveness of individual national economies can be judged in the same way as when speaking about companies.

Having said all this, when the World Economic Forum (WEF) publishes its annual ranking of countries' competitiveness, everyone pays attention. Although the rankings are primarily compiled by means of opinion surveys, they provide an indication of whether a given country's long-term growth prospects are deteriorating or improving. Even so, many have pointed out that a given country's position in the WEF ranking is only loosely related to its current economic indicators. Although a country may occupy a higher rung on the competitiveness ladder, its growth rate is not necessarily higher as a result. This is to say that competitiveness is connected not to current growth but rather to growth potential.

At the same time, the WEF's competitiveness analyses and rankings do encourage us not to limit our search for sources of sustainable growth to simply maintaining financial equilibrium and curbing (wage) costs but also to recognizing the role of investments, institutions and human resources. Of the WEF's twelve pillars of competitiveness, four (and arguably five) are closely correlated to human capital.

The question of innovation merits a separate mention. A significant change in attitude has taken place in this regard in the past decade, thanks to authors such as Mariana Mazzucato.[20] In her work, Mazzucato stresses that the state's role in capitalism today goes far beyond periodically correcting market failures. There is a tendency to regard many of the highly sophisticated products that have emerged in recent decades as achievements of private enterprise, but looking at the emblematic example of the smartphone reveals that every element of that particular invention was developed within the framework of state-sponsored innovation programmes.

In the course of the kind of wide-ranging experimentation enabled by these programmes, developers often hit upon solutions that

---

20   Mazzucato is an Italian-born professor who was educated in the US and now works in England. Her work has been popularized by the OECD and many others. Her best-known work, the 2011 economics bestseller *The Entrepreneurial State*, was already in its second edition by 2015.

they had not originally sought, since the problem itself was articulated only after the launch of the project. In such cases, then, it is not the invisible hand of the market that repeatedly generates solutions and creates economic value, but rather the hiding hand of the state – to use a phrase of Albert O. Hirschman's. The financing of these research projects is mission-oriented rather than being directly profit-oriented, and yet it indirectly promotes the accumulation of very substantial profits. In this function the state assumes a considerable portion of the financial risk of research and development, thereby significantly reducing the risk undertaken by private firms.

The resulting profits accumulated in the private sphere raise questions, however. Research connected to the extraction of shale gas, for example, has been supported by the government in the United States, and once the business based on that research was launched, the share prices of companies operating in the sector saw as much as a tenfold increase. Mazzucato proposes that, when large sums flow from state coffers into private firms for R&D purposes, the state should aim at (and would be justified in) acquiring some share of ownership in the companies it supports, precisely so that these investments earn interest directly for the public benefit.

In many respects, Mazzucato evokes the approach of earlier leading economists (such as John K. Galbraith), applying it to current actors. Her popularity may also be explained by the fact that during the financial crisis the public had already become familiar with forms of enforced state intervention, such as the recapitalization of loss-making companies or the retroactive spreading of business and systemic risks. The picture nevertheless still needs to be filled out to make the model more widely acceptable – and highlighting the state's developmental role certainly helps in this regard.[21]

Confirming her status as one of the most powerful voices in economics today, Mazzucato never neglects to emphasize that state revenues are also needed in order to cover state support for R&D – she points out, for example, that the highest tax rate in the United States at the time of NASA's foundation was 91%, and that this still

---

21 The concept of the 'developmental state' is explained by Csáki (2009) (and by Szalavetz (2009), among others).

failed to hinder economic growth and modernization. Of course, even she does not see the military–industrial complex as an optimal and indispensable incubator of development. The pull sectors have changed: today the pharmaceutical industry – or, more broadly, healthcare – has an enormous share in R&D (whether we are looking at the United States or Hungary).

Mazzucato's ideas bolster the EU's objective to raise R&D expenditures to a higher level. Increasing R&D spending is not an end in itself, but it is the main indicator of the potential of an economic development strategy. However, not all EU member countries are equally well-equipped to embark on this path unaided. The countries of the European periphery need to respond to the challenges of the 'future of work' primarily through better aligning themselves with European trends by increasing investment in human capital, an endeavour in which the EU as a community must play a guiding and supporting role. If we had to name the most relevant and positive models from among the various national economic strategies, then paradoxically we must mention in first place the example of Estonia, a country of the EU periphery. Although we cannot speak of an economic miracle in the Estonian case, its example nonetheless serves well to show that a country that recently underwent the transition from a planned economy to a market economy is not predestined for the role of an economic zone specializing in assembly plants and built on the competitiveness of cheap labour.

In many countries, the process of surveying the impact of digitalization and automation is only just beginning. Analyses being carried out within the EU, the ILO and the OECD may provide important support in shaping the future, as well as in understanding the economic and social scenarios projected by the advent of the new technological era.

OWNING TECHNOLOGY AND CREATING COMMUNITIES

Regulation, adaptation and innovation have all been elements of the public policy responses to the technological revolutions of our time, whether we are talking about the rise of robots, the spread of seemingly magical info-communication tools or the platformization of business and work. There are, however, a number of authors who are suggesting that a full answer to the challenges of new technology cannot be given without discussing alternative forms of ownership.

According to Harvard professor Richard Freeman, without partial ownership the workers can only be slaves to those who own the robots. The reflex to scrap the new machines and limit innovation almost always arises at times when a major crisis or change is brought about by technology. However, it is not from those responses that forward-looking solutions have emerged, but rather from the amalgamation of technological and social innovations, and from regulation that takes social values and needs into account.

Freeman was an early proponent of adjusting the way we manage our economic and business models. He takes the view that the present technological revolution may eventually improve the material well-being of workers, via increases in productivity leading to higher incomes and more leisure time. To achieve this, however, it is necessary for employees to have a share of the capital: to become co-owners and shareholders to a far greater extent than is the case today.

To underpin his argument, Freeman (2015) recalls the US experience with Employee Stock Ownership Plans (ESOPs). The US government introduced tax benefits for ESOPs in 1974, which helped spur a large ESOP sector that today employs around 11 million workers. Facing the challenge of technology-driven business restructuring, governments can give preferential treatment in procurement decisions to firms that meet some basic financial standard for employee ownership. But that is only one solution: given the diversity in the histories and economic structures of the advanced capitalist countries, each will have to choose the way that fits it best to extend worker ownership of capital and thereby give workers a stream of earnings from the technologies that are changing the world of work.

The need for, and the opportunity to move towards, workers' ownership is discussed in the context of the platform economy by James Muldoon (2021), who presents a vision for 'platform socialism'. He shows how grassroots communities and transnational social movements can take back control from the digital giants of neoliberal capitalism. For Muldoon, platform socialism is partly about reimagining the internet and finding alternative ways in which the ownership and governance of platforms can be organized, but it is also about the broader infrastructures and institutions that frame the economic activity of a society.

Big Tech companies deliver content to their consumers in the form of social media, creating for many the illusion of community. Pointing out the democratic deficiencies of the internet, Muldoon calls this a kind of 'community washing' that only conceals the actual novelty of these technologies: an enhanced capacity to extract information from consumers and work from employees. However, he doubts that government intervention to increase or restore market competition can be a solution on its own. While such interventions are an understandable reaction to the distortions, they are not necessarily forward-looking and may not even play a pivotal role.

To embed his analysis and vision in the socialist tradition, Muldoon invokes the thinking of authors such as the Englishman George Douglas Howard Cole and the Austrian Otto Karl Wilhelm Neurath, and he applies their pluralist socialist thought to the governance of democratic platforms. This current of socialist tradition is not in favour of the 'big state', instead representing the principle of subsidiarity and prioritizing communal and local platforms rather than monolithic technological mediators.

A century ago, 'big state' socialism bumped into the problem of calculation, frustrating the ambition of centralized economic planning.[22] This problem has been revisited by Daniel E. Saros (2014), who has outlined how modern information technology can be used to implement a new method of economic calculation. Socialist

---

22 Following World War I and the socialist revolutions of Central and Eastern Europe, conservative Austrian economists (such as Ludwig von Mises and Friedrich Hayek) gave serious thought to the complexity of the calculation that would be needed to run a planned economy based on state ownership, and they identified this as a major obstacle to socialism. In later decades in the Soviet Union and elsewhere, computerization and mathematical modelling was developed with the intention of optimizing the planning system. In principle, the availability of high-capacity computers together with advanced data management and AI allows us to revisit today a century-old debate about the feasibility of socialist economic planning.

economic models have to incorporate the benefits of information technology, and the genuinely new methods of calculation that are available could help bring about an end to capitalism and make socialism possible. Saros thus proposes an entirely new model of socialist development, based on a 'needs profile' that makes it possible to convert the needs of human communities into data that can be used as a guide for resource allocation.

For Evgeny Morozov (2019), Saros's 'overall vision provides inspiration and encouragement to those searching for alternative ways of coordinating economic activity on a large scale'. Morozov himself exposes the ostensible megatrend of digitalization as a facade to privatization and the general shift to a free-market model. The 'datafication' of everyday life is an extension of the much broader phenomenon of its financialization. The counter-trend must aim at socializing the data and creating platforms that give priority to human objectives over the maximization of profits. Progress should be defined not on the basis of finding 'smart solutions' to all aspects of production and services under the rules of a market economy, but in terms of breaking the exclusive property of tech giants over the means for creating alternative modes of social coordination (the 'feedback infrastructure').

Morozov's 2014 classic *To Save Everything, Click Here: The Folly of Technological Solutionism* challenges the widespread rhetoric of techno-optimism, or digital utopianism, and explains why technological development alone cannot resolve social problems. His critique of 'solutionism' calls for technological progress to be analysed from a perspective embedded in political economy. The point does not relate only to public services, health, education or culture: it is that digital solutionism did not work out for financial capitalism either. Indeed, in the wake of the great global liberalization of the 1990s, the computerization of financial management helped to create the illusion of risk-free transnational investments, which backfired at the time of the 2008 meltdown.

Just as Mazzucato destroys the notion that neoliberalism is the key to value creation in the digital era, Morozov destroys the arguments suggesting that neoliberalism is the key to the fair distribution of that value. What is expressed here is not technophobia but the need to ensure that new technology is developed and applied with the objective of serving the satisfaction of genuine human needs instead of enhancing the capacity to extract ever-greater profits for privileged groups.

The social dimension and political cohesion

DANGERS OF DISINTEGRATION

The financial and economic crises of 2008–13 eroded, and in certain countries even severely undermined, confidence in European integration. This was principally because the European Union appeared to many not as a force protecting society from financial upheaval but as a potential threat to livelihoods, local self-determination and social cohesion. As the recovery began, however, support for the EU also returned, and once again the conviction spread that the Union needed to be strengthened if European countries were to prosper. That being said, there can be no strengthening of the EU without expanding its social dimension.

A 2012 World Bank report on the European economic model highlighted just what was at stake in such changes in attitude. The lengthy study, titled 'Golden growth', acknowledged the special achievements of European economic and social progress, particularly in the area of convergence (i.e. the bridging of the gap between the centre and the regions of the periphery). It characterized the EU as a 'lifestyle superpower', which was regarded in many other parts of the world as a better model to follow than the United States. At the same time, the World Bank's experts urged that measures be taken to ensure the sustainability of this growth model, emphasizing the importance of innovation capacity, labour mobility and demographic challenges. As for the euro (which had been dancing on the edge of the abyss for years), the other Washington institution – the International Monetary Fund (IMF) – had been constantly raising its voice for the currency's reform in this period.

That the main trend in the EU's immediate future might actually prove to be its diminishment rather than its strengthening was the message sent by the outcome of the European Parliament elections of 2014 (which saw various nationalist, populist and Eurosceptic forces noticeably bolstered). Then followed the double shock of 2016: the result of the Brexit referendum and the election of Donald Trump as US president. The co-occurrence of these two events led many to declare the advent of some kind of populist megatrend; this perception had simultaneous dispiriting and stimulating effects on the EU, on its cohesion and on the ongoing efforts to strengthen it. The Brexit process created persistent economic uncertainty within the United Kingdom, but it also increased the chances of the EU placing greater emphasis on previously neglected (or frustrated) concerns, such as the adherence to political and social norms. These concerns were duly elaborated in the course of 2016–17.

If the twenty-seven member countries remaining after the British departure wished to develop a stable, sustainable order and functioning EU mechanisms, then they could not rely on the knee-jerk reactions, fatalism and passions that burst forth from UK debates around the referendum. These debates were far removed from reality, as pro-leave campaigners often deliberately exaggerated the costs of membership, particularly in relation to matters such as internal EU migration. On other questions, however, such as the transparency and democratic control of EU institutions, they pointed to genuine contradictions that occupied the attention of others as well.

Almost everywhere in continental Europe, Brexit is painted as a loss for both sides (although the British are probably losing a lot more than the twenty-seven countries that remained). The Germans and Dutch have lost an important trading partner, while the Scandinavian countries have lost an ally who was similarly opposed to the deepening of the EU. The Italians are sorry to see the weakening of the counterweight to the German–French axis. From the perspective of the Visegrád countries, the endangering of the jobs of many of their citizens represents a significant loss, and that is coupled with the fear that the departure of a net contributing country puts pressure on the EU budget and reduces the amount of funding for development.

The most important of Brexit's long-term implications in terms of integration is that it represents the departure of a country that was always opposed to ever-closer integration. With few exceptions, members have always valued the economic importance of the EU far more highly than its political importance, and this was especially true for Britain. At the same time, Britain's departure has been interpreted in the remaining twenty-seven member countries as being more of an reckless misstep than a viable, constructive response to real problems. Not only has the trend towards disintegration seen no acceleration, the populist tide has even started to wane. The strengthening, adjustment and improved operation of the EU have become goals of the twenty-seven member states, and these goals have accordingly provided common social policy with an opportunity and room for manoeuvre.

Initially, however, the nationalist and populist tendencies that flared in the wake of the profound and prolonged financial crisis were taken by many to signify that further progress in integration was impossible since its support among society was lacking (or at least dwindling). This growing uncertainty – and the paralysing effect of the Brexit referendum – was also reflected in a White Paper published by the European Commission in March 2017 that addressed the debates over the future of Europe. The discussion paper looked at the changes Europe would face over the next decade (from the impact of new technologies reshaping society and jobs to doubts relating to globalization, security concerns and the spread of populism). As the document put it, either the EU drifts with the tide or it turns these processes to its own benefit, taking advantage of the new, latent opportunities.

The document placed great emphasis on the demographic situation, as well as on the decline in the EU's relative economic weight. Noting that by 2060 not one of the EU's member states will account for even as much as 1% of the world's population, it also characterized this demographic change as a compelling argument for staying together, since more can be achieved as a group: 'A positive global force, Europe's prosperity will continue to depend on its openness and strong links with its partners.' Besides vividly illustrating the interdependence of member countries, the White Paper also opened up debate over a number of directions (formalized as a set of scenarios) that might enable the partial rollback of the EU.[23] This dismantlement could potentially occur either by grouping certain countries into a more loosely connected 'outer circle' or through the Union scaling back its powers in individual areas that were judged less important from the perspective of integration (with common examples being regional development, healthcare, social affairs and defence policy).

A number of individual authors have confronted this lack of self-confidence and the near-defeatist mood, among them Giles Merritt. Even the title of the veteran journalist's book – *Slippery Slope: Europe's Troubled Future* – sounds depressing. However, Merritt adopts a position in opposition to the fashionable clichés of political scientists: in his view, it is not that the EU has over-stretched itself, but that it is too timid. He sees the member countries as insufficiently decisive in seeking answers to shared, largely global challenges in a unified way (meaning with the aid of EU institutions) or in concentrating their resources to the extent necessary to achieve this (which would be far greater than at present). Merritt envisages no master plan; instead he sees a series of many small steps to be assembled into a flexible programme for the revitalization of the EU. The elements he conceives include the more rational development of infrastructure, the elevation of certain elements of the welfare safety net to the Union level, and the promotion of digitalization (and the training required for it). He also envisages a broader mandate for the ECB (based on the US model) – although, as he puts it, this too requires no revolution, simply rational decision-making.

---

23 The eye-catching titles of Juncker's five scenarios were (1) 'Carrying on', (2) 'Nothing but the single market', (3) 'Those who want more do more', (4) 'Doing less more efficiently' and (5) 'Doing much more together'. Of these, scenario (3) was interpreted by many as a vision for detaching the east-ern member countries. In truth, however, Juncker was discussing not two separate groups of countries (first and second class, or outer and inner circles) but overlapping areas of thematic cooperation, for which the Treaty provides the opportunity to this day. If this were to become the general model, then several such groupings might emerge, with those remaining outside no longer able to 'hold captive' those who demand a deeper form of integration.

Since EU decision-making amid the network of interests of the twenty-seven members can be very slow indeed (with even small reforms often requiring a long time to reach fruition), meaningful action is usually triggered not by gradually weakening performance but only by existential crises.

REFOCUSING EU SOCIAL POLICY

Jean-Claude Juncker's White Paper was followed by further reflection papers, one of which dealt with the EU's social dimension. The debate over social policy that was sparked half-way through the Juncker Commission clearly reflected the general sense of uncertainty. While the reflection paper on the social dimension did not cleave to the methods and objectives of the Europe 2020 Strategy, there was little clarity around what should replace them or whether the EU's social dimension should apply to all member countries or only to those of the eurozone.

After the Europe 2020 Strategy was launched in 2010, the so-called European Semester framework synchronized the economic and social dimensions of community governance, taking into account the National Reform Programmes prepared by the individual member countries. Within the social dimension, a new balance was established between labour affairs and social protection. This was because the Strategy contained among its seven flagship initiatives the Platform against Poverty, which included a specific target number with respect to reducing poverty and social exclusion (at least 20 million people by 2020). Simultaneously, social policy appeared explicitly in the Employment Guidelines (which urged 'promoting social inclusion and combating poverty').

When drawing up the Europe 2020 Strategy, it was clear that much more needed to be done to combat unemployment and poverty (including youth unemployment and child poverty). Each member country had to set numerically measurable goals to help the common programme become a reality. What the Commission failed to reckon with in 2010 was the protracted euro crisis. For this reason, a number of member countries not only were unable to make advances towards the 2020 targets but even suffered a worsening of their problems. Even the better performers saw a slowdown in their progress.

Under the aegis of the Strategy, a number of important documents were delivered to operationalize the programme in specific areas while complementing it in the context of the eurozone crisis that had deepened in the meantime.[24] During this period, the Commission left no stone unturned in their review of every aspect of welfare models: it made recommendations for combating child poverty, it provided methodological support for the creation of minimum income schemes and the eradication of homelessness, it introduced the youth guarantee programme (which facilitated the elimination of joblessness lasting more than four months for the under-twenty-fives), it offered guidance to social enterprises (including on how to make efficient use of EU funds for social policy purposes), and it brought in new rules to protect the rights of migrant workers. At the same time, the relationship between the EU's financial instruments and the social policies of member states also underwent change. Implementing the new concepts in practice entailed updating legislation and renewing budgetary instruments.[25]

Despite these steps by the Commission, the more active EU social policy was overshadowed by a macroeconomic policy that favoured fiscal rigour, and it was this policy that provided the framework for overall crisis management in the 2010–12 period and that led to controversial outcomes. During this period, it was often heard (sometimes even from holders of high political office) that, while Europe provides only 8% of the world's population and produces only a quarter of the world's total GDP, the continent accounts

---

24   Those interested in the Europe 2020 Strategy and EU social policy of the crisis period can refer to the following EU documents: the EU Framework for National Roma Integration Strategies (2011), the White Paper on Pensions (2012), the Employment Package (2012), the Youth Employment Package (2012) and the Social Investment Package (2013).

25   After much debate, the EU budget for 2014–20 stipulated that at least 20% of the European Social Fund must be dedicated to promoting social inclusion. In addition, it retained – and even reinforced – the Fund for European Aid to the Most Deprived (FEAD), a scheme providing food to those most in need. In January 2013 the European Council set aside €6 billion in the 2014–20 framework budget to support the youth guarantee.

for as much as 50% of the world's total social expenditures. These statistics allow the easy conclusion to be reached that a responsible policy must dampen welfare spending – in the interests of everyone's future. This discourse is an example of how economic policy can adopt fashionable themes, and how maxims and slogans supported by neither theory nor experience sometimes enter into vogue.

To determine the true value of such wisdom, we need to know exactly what the quoted numbers contain. The figures cited above under the name of welfare expenditures, for example, do not include healthcare spending, although many would regard this as self-evidently belonging to the welfare system. This is a very important consideration, as healthcare in the United States costs significantly more than it does in Europe. If we therefore add together all realistically relevant welfare expenditures (thus also including funds dedicated to healthcare), the EU's share of the world's combined social spending immediately drops from 50% to only 40%.

Among countries with developed economies it is not only common but practically the rule for substantial sums to be spent on social purposes. OECD data clearly show that EU member countries and the United States dedicate similar amounts to social expenditures: approximately a quarter of GDP. This level can be regarded as commonplace in the most developed countries of the world; it is essentially an inherent sign of development, and not some kind of deviation from the norm.

The quibbling over welfare expenditures – besides leading to confusing conclusions based on unclear data – diverts attention away from the real obstacles to progress: luxury consumption, for example, or a significant portion of various prestige investment projects, but also corruption. While waste really does need to be prevented, it would be wrong to cite this as a pretext for trimming the amounts given to community funds dedicated to primary education, or care of children and the elderly.

It was in order to clarify the above issues that the European Commission adopted a document in February 2013 with the name of the Social Investment Package (SIP), which provided an impetus to common thinking and concrete efforts in social policy among the member countries. This document portrayed social investment as the kind of investment that always pays out a reliable return. The SIP guidance asserted that the building of modern welfare states based on social investment serves two objectives of the Europe 2020 Strategy at once: reducing poverty and increasing the rate of employment.

How do we protect the most important social expenditures for the future in a time of budgetary consolidation? What are the best strategies available to the EU for combating homelessness? How can social enterprises help, and how can EU funds be used most effectively for social policy goals? It is to these and similar questions that the SIP endeavoured to provide answers. It also made it unequivocally clear that the causes of the crisis that was afflicting many European countries were not to be sought in social policy. Nevertheless, the modernization of welfare states is vital if we are to avoid the more serious social harms while also furthering economic recovery. In this spirit, all incidences of scapegoating those on the margins of society for the difficulties faced by the community as a whole are unacceptable. Despite today's difficult circumstances, the programme of job creation and social integration must not be abandoned; instead, new tools must be sought for its implementation. The EU's council of labour ministers (EPSCO) took a decision in support of social investment when it adopted the youth guarantee programme in February 2013 – a programme that facilitated the elimination of joblessness lasting more than four months for the under-twenty-fives.

The change of attitude embodied in the concept of social investment holds that welfare policy must not simply act as retroactive compensation for harm (i.e. social protection) but must also lay the foundations for better performance in the future. Though a time of crisis may mean that governments have fewer resources at their disposal to directly remedy ever-deepening inequalities, they do have the possibility – and indeed the obligation – to take action in favour of equal opportunities. The type of redistribution that offers a leg up to those who are lagging behind and enables them to participate in economic and social life is precisely what constitutes 'social investment'. Strengthening this redistribution in the short and long term alike can have a beneficial impact on employment, productivity and social cohesion. If we specify a portion of GDP to be dedicated to social investment, we will save ourselves considerable social and economic expenditures in future. Examples of such investment include the introduction of programmes such as the youth guarantee, the development of quality child care services that also help parents get back to work, the prevention of disease and child poverty, and the promotion of quality education and active ageing.

Although it was their economic models, and not their social models, that plunged European countries into a deep crisis, this does not mean that social models face no factors that would compel reform (to name a few: economic cycles, long-term demographic trends, and changes in the organization of labour brought about by technological progress). Maintaining strong welfare states depends on their capacity for adaptation and renewal. The notion of social investment is intended to provide a conceptual framework for this forward-looking reform.

DELIVERING THE SOCIAL PILLAR

After the European Parliament elections of 2014, European society – having been put to the test by prolonged crises – awaited confirmation that the EU's social dimension was still something that would be taken seriously. For this reason, the new president of the European Commission, Jean-Claude Juncker, declared that he would do all in his power to help the EU achieve a triple-A rating on social issues. It took a long time, however, to decide which specific initiatives would ensure such a rating.

Early 2016 saw the announcement of a public consultation on the European Pillar of Social Rights, which took up the best part of the year. During this time the Commission drew up a summary of the pillar and an inventory of its specifics, declaring that the consultation process might lead to reviews, adjustments or the introduction of new instruments in certain areas. The European Parliament engaged in the debate, with Maria João Rodrigues playing a pivotal role as rapporteur. The Social Pillar included twenty principles against which the social models of individual member countries, and the performance and quality thereof, might be judged (covering education, healthcare, the youth guarantee, social dialogue and care for the elderly, among other areas).

The European Union cannot be regarded merely as a continent-wide marketplace. It is a social market economy, and for very specific reasons: social rights are protected by a substantial portion of the EU acquis; social investments form significant expenditures in the EU budget; and social dialogue is assigned an important role in EU governance, meaning that representatives of employers and employees alike have an important say in the key decisions that affect them.

Since European systems of welfare provision are not managed by the EU itself, welfare expenditures predominantly form a part of individual members' national budgets, and it will always prove difficult at the EU level to adopt initiatives aimed at 'solving' social problems (such as homelessness). At the same time, part of the EU's credibility depends on it paying attention to the social problems of member countries, regions and communities. It needs to bear these in mind when exercising its other powers (e.g. in macroeconomic decision-making or market regulation), when distributing its own funds and when assessing fulfilment of cohesion and convergence targets within the Union.

Initially, the scope of the Social Pillar applied not to the entire EU but to only the eurozone countries (with it remaining optional for those outside the zone). This lenient approach – predating the Brexit referendum of 2016 – was designed to forestall any anti-Brussels reaction among British public opinion. However, it proved to be a problematic approach anyway, since the EU as a whole, just as it needs to present a united front over human rights, must do the same with respect to social rights. One theoretical explanation for narrowing the pillar's application to the eurozone might have been that the intensification of alarming social problems in the EU over the previous decade had happened mostly in the eurozone, and especially on its southern periphery (which had particular problems with soaring unemployment, poverty and income inequalities). The divergence of the periphery from the centre was well illustrated by the Social Scoreboard first introduced in 2013.

The Social Pillar was 'solemnly proclaimed' at an informal summit in the Swedish city of Gothenburg in November 2017. Besides heads of state and government and leaders of EU institutions, heads of employers' and workers' organizations were also present, as well as representatives of social NGOs. The contents of the document were arranged in three main chapters: 'Equal opportunities and access to the labour market', 'Fair working conditions' and 'Social protection and inclusion'. The document was then printed in the form of a little blue booklet in every official language of the EU.

The launch of the Social Pillar was clearly meant to be a declaration of principle, its initiators aiming to avoid even the appearance of wishing to transform the EU into a common welfare state. At the same time, the social market economy as described in EU treaties also means the EU cannot ignore the social consequences of economic integration or of competition within the European market. Indeed, the legislative, political and budgetary tools to help strengthen national social models have been part of the operations of the Union from the outset. One more tool came in 2017, when the Juncker Commission – building on earlier similar initiatives – deemed it necessary to relaunch the Social Scoreboard. Incorporated into the European Semester, this tool was designed to help fine-tune economic governance. It was also clear that the body of social policy legislation that had formed in the 1990s needed updating in several respects. Over the years since the EU encircled the newly created single market with a protective ring of social legislation, the world of work – and the structure of labour markets – has transformed. Globalization has unfolded in the world economy, while the new technologies of digitalization and automation have shifted the organization of work towards even greater flexibility.

However, the European Commission likes to play it safe, and while it moved mountains in the debates over the Social Pillar, the 2017 social package contained only one new legislative initiative, which was aimed at better reconciling working time with private life. The Commission urged every EU member country to introduce paternity leave, envisaging its positive impact in both the economic and demographic spheres. Beyond slogans, this would be a concrete step towards equality between men and women.

Nevertheless, cohesion cannot be created only from values, norms and rules: it requires tangible, material acts of solidarity to be undertaken within a community. In many countries, the rhetorical elevation of a social agenda can exert only a limited impact in the absence of simultaneous reform elsewhere (e.g. currency union, regulation of the financial system or a cohesion policy aiding convergence).

The effectiveness of welfare models and policies is greatly dependent on how much society is able to control and adequately regulate the trends, processes and above all economic policy decisions that fall outside the scope of social policy. Specifically, the feasibility of euro reform is a fundamental question for the EU from the perspective of cohesion, as is the further convergence of the eastern peripheral region without – or with the reversal of – the internal polarization experienced so far. Both cases presuppose a degree of solidarity greater than has been seen before, as well as joint action against inequalities and imbalances. The Social Pillar will have a positive effect provided that it helps define what the EU community wishes to achieve in the areas of labour and welfare via the reforms and coordinative measures it has initiated.

Conceptually, the Social Pillar harks back to the period of the establishment of the European single market, when Jacques Delors first shaped the EU's social dimension. It was the 1989 Social Charter that placed the focus on social rights, albeit typically grouping those rights around the world of work, in line with the common interests of social partners (i.e. employers and workers). Nevertheless, it serves well to illustrate well the evolution in thinking that, while the 1989 Charter began with the right to freedom of movement, over the course of a quarter of a century the emphasis shifted towards the right to equal access to the labour market and towards the training and investment in human capital that facilitate successful employment.

The advantage of a social dimension shaped around rights is that it connects to the concepts and language of universal human rights. Another consequence is that it is not necessary to deal with the material implications of how those particular rights would be fulfilled. However, the concept then becomes open to attack, since most of the declared social rights – from fair wages to education to housing – entail some material aspect, and for this reason debate can arise over when certain rights are attainable and when they are not. The declaration of rights essentially becomes only a vision.

At the time of the 2019 European Parliament elections, much uncertainty surrounded the Social Pillar and its future. It is not uncommon for a paradigm and a set of programmes introduced by one Commission to be simply shunted aside, sunk or gutted by its successor.

Significant social and political forces have nevertheless mobilized in defence of the Social Pillar. The viability of the paradigm was shown when the expression 'social rights' first appeared at the naming of the members of the new European Commission in 2019.

SOCIAL DIALOGUE AND FAIR WAGES

One visible impact of the Social Pillar was that it increased the attention paid to certain issues at the EU level, thereby prompting the elevation of debates over topics such as wages that would have been unimaginable a decade or two earlier. Prior to the 2019 European Parliament elections, European trade unions had run a campaign under the slogan 'Europe needs a pay rise.' The issue became even more salient because many saw it as a constructive extension of the social dumping debate of the Juncker era that the EU was beginning to discuss the convergence of wage levels in the countries of the periphery.

In the legal sense, the EU has no direct competence in the area of wage formation. Although social models differ from country to country and from region to region, social partners have indispensable roles, important scopes of action and established rights almost everywhere. Chief among those established rights is that wages should be negotiated and agreed upon in the context of collective bargaining. The idea of wage coordination at the EU level therefore encountered substantial debate and had to deal with serious objections.

At the same time, adoption of the Social Pillar has opened up the possibility for debate on the issue of wages at the EU level. If the EU's competence were to extend to wages (whether by establishing wage levels or by choosing a mechanism for determining them), it would represent a genuinely new element – and yet a new element that would have its antecedents amid the turmoil of the crisis management after 2010.[26] If the EU were to proceed within the framework of the

---

26   In the Employment Package of 2012, the Commission initiated the establishment of a minimum wage in every member country (long before this appeared in the official government programme in Germany). Minimum wage levels in Greece were impacted by the conditionality of the EU–IMF loans it was granted, while country-specific recommendations (for example, in the case of Belgium and Cyprus) also contained reviews of wage-setting mechanisms.

Social Pillar, determining a mandatory, common methodology that applied to all member states, this would not mean that the EU would actually take over the task of determining wages. What it would mean is that lower-income countries, where lower wages represent a competitive advantage from the outset, would be obliged to protect workers from impoverishment. For a significant number of workers, this is the point where convergence either stands or falls – the point where it either remains a mirage or becomes a genuine possibility. Put simply, the EU is calling members to account for fulfilment of a contractually stated goal, linked to a common programme that the member states together agreed upon in the summer of 2010: namely, the Europe 2020 Strategy and the struggle against poverty.

A universal European minimum wage, set in absolute terms at a certain value, obviously does not make sense. If a prescribed level is workable in Bulgaria, then it offers nothing to the Dutch. If it is relevant in Denmark, then it will kill competitiveness in Poland. But if we think of relative, not absolute, minimum wage levels – meaning that we seek the optimal minimum wage level compared with the average wage – then it makes sense to think in terms of common methods and common wage brackets. Statistics show that, among European countries, a higher minimum wage (amounting to 45–50% of the average wage) not only offers better protection against poverty but also brings a higher rate of employment among the low-skilled and women. A jointly elaborated European minimum-wage-setting methodology, to be followed in all member states, might place domestic debates and negotiations back on a constructive track. However, marking out a new kind of developmental trajectory requires new member countries not to simply raise the lowest wages but also to strengthen genuine social dialogue. A shift to a neo-corporatist model that is seen as more successful for Europe as a whole – and competitive in the context of the global economy – might also bring substantial benefits to East-Central Europe in particular.

However, wage levels are a matter not simply of subsistence and convergence but also of the long-term stability of currency union. Wages that continuously evolve independently of productivity may lead to imbalances and exacerbate crises, making the latter even more costly for workers and taxpayers alike. Consequently, much attention is being paid in Brussels – following the inspiration of

André Sapir – to the establishment of so-called competitiveness councils. The creation of these councils in member countries was initiated by the Commission back in 2015, after the Five Presidents' Report summarized the structural problems of monetary union and mapped out directions for coordinated action. Naturally, there are certainly some who see this more as a coordinated substitute for action, since the EU does not generally struggle with problems of competitiveness, but rather with internal imbalances.

In terms of specific solutions, greater coordination of wage dynamics would be one key to eliminating existing imbalances at the eurozone level. For the eurozone, the question is primarily not one of a debt crisis but one of a crisis in demand – and if this crisis is to be averted, it requires new tools to expand investment, as well as assistance in raising low incomes. If we take this as a starting point, then the EU might also need to think about setting up 'demand councils' alongside the competitiveness councils. While it is true that we are accustomed to seeing wage costs (at the level of individual firms) as one of the main factors in competitiveness, wage developments are also important on the macroeconomic level because of their impact on aggregate demand. If everyone in Europe wished to increase competitiveness by holding back wages, then it would have roughly the same effect as if everyone were to simultaneously devalue their national currency – and everyone would lose in the end.

The trajectory of the debate over coordination of the minimum wage at the EU level was influenced by the fundamental change in mainstream opinion and practice in Germany in the 2010s. The significance of the German minimum wage that was introduced in 2015 goes far beyond Germany and its lowest-income strata. For a long time, the Germans (including German trade unions) did not wish to even countenance the introduction of a minimum wage. The fact that it was finally introduced can be counted as a joint achievement of the parties that governed together in the 'grand coalition' at the time of its implementation. Opinion leaders who previously cautioned Germany against the dangers of the minimum wage now have to grit their teeth and acknowledge that its introduction has not entailed any sacrifice of employment opportunities. German joblessness has steadily declined over time, even in a year of a positive supply shock such as 2015, although in the latter case the continuation of the positive trend was partly due to the huge surplus demand for labour created by the refugee crisis in areas such as language teaching, vocational training, public security and social services.

The successful introduction of a minimum wage in Germany provides an incentive for the creation of a common, EU-wide methodology for determining minimum wage levels among member states.[27] In 2020 – the first year of the Covid pandemic – the European Commission officially launched an initiative to guarantee a sufficient minimum wage across all member states. One year later both the European Parliament and the Council voiced their support, giving confidence to those who had expected a favourable outcome for the initiative. And then in June 2022, before the French presidency of the Council came to a close, Parliament and Council finally agreed on the text of the directive that obliges the member states to take care of the adequacy of minimum wages and promote collective bargaining for that purpose

HOUSING AS A NEW FRONTIER

The issues of housing and homelessness serve as good examples of how, in certain instances, the Social Pillar has not necessarily provided an impetus to the resolution of urgent problems. The 2017 declaration of social rights left open the questions of whose task it is to lead the search for a solution and what specific resources they would have at their disposal. Although the nineteenth point of the Social Pillar stipulates the right to adequate housing conditions, including assistance for members of vulnerable groups, it does not provide anyone with any specific new powers or resources that would be directed at achieving this.

At the same time, FEANTSA (the European federation of non-governmental organizations working with the homeless) believes that Europe already has the means at its disposal to help countries cope with the problems of homelessness. The EU manages initiatives such as the Urban Agenda and the Social Pillar that could serve as launch pads

---

27   For Germany's experience with the minimum wage and the feasibility of minimum wage coordination at the EU level, see Luebker and Schulten (2022).

for protecting the right to housing, or that could offer support through financial means – partly from EU funds. However, FEANTSA would also like to see EU bodies adopt a Europe-wide strategy specifically for this purpose, and the NGO has convinced many of this necessity via successful lobbying efforts targeted at the European Parliament and the European Economic and Social Committee (EESC).

Although the EU has yet to draw up an official document defined as a common EU strategy (and bearing this in its title), the past decade has seen the community take steps in this direction. Financial support is to be earmarked for local housing initiatives, while regional development funds have been available for housing purposes since 2009. Direct EU financing, for example, supported the cooperation of railway companies in eliminating homelessness at railway stations in a humane manner in order to provide better support for those affected.

Of the nine elements that form the indicator measuring material deprivation used within the framework of the Europe 2020 Strategy, two are directly connected to housing (problems with loan repayments or housing-related payment arrears; a lack of adequate heating), while a further three relate to the quality of the dwelling (whether financial reasons have caused the occupier to lack a telephone, colour television or washing machine). These examples illustrate that, although a common strategy is yet to be drawn up at the EU level, documents that relate to the social dimension routinely touch on the issue of improving housing conditions and the struggle against homelessness. The Commission has also made it unequivocally clear that the criminalization of homelessness is unacceptable.

The 2013 Social Investment Package (SIP) contained a working document that provided a comprehensive analysis of the causes of homelessness in EU member countries and that called for concrete strategic measures to counter them. Over many pages it discussed the possibilities for prevention, distinguishing the factors that increase the risk of homelessness from those that actually trigger it. It also listed the EU resources that could be used in the struggle against homelessness and to improve housing conditions (e.g. reducing energy poverty).

The SIP – in keeping with EU custom – also dealt with the identification of 'good practices'. A consensus exists in social policy that the best strategy is application of the 'street to home' Housing First model used in Finland and, earlier, in London and Glasgow. The essence of this model is best illustrated by a description of the alternative, whereby the homeless are initially placed in homeless shelters and often remain there for extended periods. Even in better-financed cases, this type of accommodation does not lead easily to lasting recovery: instead it tends to ensure only survival and access to primary healthcare. In its working document, the Commission threw in its lot with the 'street to home' model.

The sole blemish of the working document (at least from the point of view of NGOs) is that it was issued as an annex to a communication of the European Commission and not as a communication in its own right. It therefore represented the Commission's technocratic position but without inviting the Council and European Parliament to support that position politically, or asserting that the EU wishes to move to deploy the tools at its disposal and launch joint action. At the same time, the working document does assist all member states that wish to develop their own strategies to deal with homelessness. The greater problem is that since 2013 there has been no fresh focus on the issue of homelessness as a separate set of tasks to be tackled.

Following the long years of crisis, it is no surprise that, with few exceptions, the numbers of the homeless have swollen in all EU member countries. Although Finland is one welcome exception, the situation has deteriorated badly in many major cities, and particularly in Southern Europe; in Athens, statistics list every seventieth resident as being homeless (according to 2017 data). While Finland is among the highest-income EU member states and Greece among the most unfortunate victims of the crisis (and of its creditors), the list of severe cases also includes countries such as the United Kingdom (in twentieth place in the pre-Brexit EU-28 ranking), which certainly could not be considered one of the poorer European countries. In itself, therefore, a country's income level does not determine its citizens' access to housing. Much is due to the nature of the social welfare system and its ability to withstand shocks.

Just as can be seen with other social problems, young people are more severely hit by homelessness and housing problems than are the population on average. In 2017, some 65% of young people in

Germany, 78% in Denmark and 58% in the United Kingdom spent more than 40% of their income on housing. At the same time, in places that saw the arrival of many more people from abroad during the crisis period, the proportion of migrants among the homeless rose significantly (in London, for example, around 20% of those registered as homeless in 2016 were Romanian citizens). Nevertheless, how much responsibility the EU has to bear for the rise of homelessness during the crisis remains an open question. In this context, we also have to ask whether the EU could provide more direct support in future to reduce or even eliminate homelessness.

From a practical point of view, the 2013 working document might serve as a starting point for determining areas of responsibility and developing new initiatives. For example, we might declare that steps should be taken at the EU level to reduce the risk of homelessness, while cooperation among stakeholders within member countries (such as regions, local governments and NGOs) should play the main role in the provision of care. It is important for the EU to devote more than just one substantial document per decade to the issue. At the same time, it must be recognized that one of the main areas in which risks can be reduced is the better regulation of the financial system (and especially more effective protection of families in the event of mortgage repayment difficulties) – assuming the political will exists to achieve this.

A GREEN DEAL AND A JUST TRANSITION

The 2019 election period saw a revival of the green agenda in the European Union. When Jean-Claude Juncker entered office five years earlier, he abolished the autonomous environment and climate portfolios in the European Commission. Environment was merged with maritime affairs and fisheries, while climate was merged with energy. In 2019, the protection of the climate became the number one policy issue of the incoming Commission headed by Ursula von der Leyen. The European Green Deal it went on to launch was seen as the start of a new era and as a clarion call for a real turnaround in economic and social development in Europe. The Green Deal enjoyed support across the board, even if distinct doubts remained about the capacity of the European Commission to achieve what was necessary in this field.

One reason for scepticism was that, while in past decades – and in the preceding year in particular – the demand for progressive ecological policies carried the title 'Green New Deal' (Pettifor 2019), the EU's policy was developed as simply a 'Green Deal'. Since this would be the first such Green Deal, it could be argued that including 'New' was superfluous. However, the point is that the earlier phrase – beyond describing a deal that would be both green and new – specifically implied a call for a green update of the New Deal, the famous policy launched and implemented by US President Franklin D. Roosevelt in response to the Great Depression of the 1930s. While it is well known that Roosevelt's New Deal introduced bank regulation, public works and federal unemployment insurance, what is less frequently mentioned is that it was also intended to be green. Roosevelt invested massively in soil conservation to stop erosion and save farmland (through the creation of the Soil Conservation Service), and he shifted the energy mix towards renewable sources (namely hydropower, through creation of the Tennessee Valley Authority), while his Civilian Conservation Corps planted more than 2 billion trees – around the same number planted throughout all of US history up to that point. All this would not have been possible without stepping up government intervention in the economy, and this is exactly what we should highlight here.

Why do we talk about a green transition by borrowing a phrase created in 1933 in the United States? It is because we do not trust the contemporary capitalist system alone to reconcile economic productivity with ecological sustainability and social justice. As state intervention has been pushed back since the 1980s, so inequality has grown and climate change has become a paramount issue for humanity. Dropping the 'New' from the Green New Deal signals a lack of understanding of the need to draw the curtain on the neoliberal era if we are serious about meeting our social and ecological objectives. The majority of Europeans, and European youth in particular, demand a new direction. This sentiment has been expressed through many demonstrations and protests, and it also made itself felt in the European Parliament elections of 2019.

In any event, even if the word 'New' was not included on this occasion, the European Green Deal appeared as an admirable attempt to provide a vision and framework for action. Of course, environmental and climate policies are not new in the EU, but they were never foremost in decision makers' minds, or at least they were not as mainstream as they are today. By contrast, the European Green Deal has been positioned as the EU's flagship initiative and is structurally embedded in everything the Union does. All other policies (in energy, transportation, agriculture, taxation, urban development and so forth) will have to be made consistent with the initiative and with its long-term climate objectives. It is the task of the commissioner in charge – First Vice-President of the European Commission Frans Timmermans – to ensure this happens.

The 2050 climate neutrality objective and the EU's recent commitment to reduce greenhouse gas emissions by at least 55% by 2030 compared with 1990 are orientation points that help European citizens and economic actors alike understand the direction of travel, providing some measure of predictability in this unpredictable world so as to secure investments in the carbon-neutral economy of tomorrow.

After its first big initiative of publishing the European Green Deal communication in December 2019, the European Commission launched an impressive number of strategies and action plans over the course of 2020 on each of the core building blocks of the Green Deal. These strategies and plans address most of the key systems that define the way we live and work, from the food system and biodiversity to mobility, the built environment and the circular economy. Some cross-sectoral issues have been partially addressed via the introduction of the Just Transition Mechanism and the Sustainable Europe Investment Plan, for example. Meanwhile, the Multiannual Financial Framework (the EU budget for the 2021–7 period) earmarks 30% of the total budget to be used for climate action.

Most importantly, the European Climate Law provides the architecture and mechanisms that should keep the EU on track as it heads towards climate neutrality, with a system of five-yearly updates that offer an opportunity to see where we are and to readjust policies where needed. This five-yearly review should not be left in the hands of a few Commission officials or the Council. One possible solution is to create a European version of the Intergovernmental Panel on Climate Change (IPCC), which would bring the scientific community and experts into the discussion in an interdisciplinary way in order to facilitate a more transparent, publicly debated assessment.

Policies to protect the climate are closely meshed with social questions on many points, so much so that the fight against climate change depends to a great extent on the success of the fight against inequality. It has been established that, globally, the richest 1% of the population is responsible for twice as many greenhouse gas emissions as the poorest half of humanity, and that it has a carbon footprint 100 times greater. On the other hand, pushing back or phasing out environmentally harmful economic activities threatens millions of jobs. Due to the awareness of this inevitable transformation combined with the simultaneous lack of clarity about transformational policies, a considerable number of people remain unsure if any future economic prosperity would include a place for them. 'Leaving nobody behind' cannot just be a slogan: it must be a central element of climate policy, and it must also take up a much more prominent position at the heart of EU Green Deal policymaking (El Khadraoui 2021).

It is not only climate change but also certain transition policies that can have uneven effects on people depending on their economic situation and social status. Subsidies for buying electric cars or installing solar panels are clearly used more by people who can afford to make such investments. By contrast, poorer people spend a larger share of their budgets on energy. Many will surely oppose change if it creates or aggravates inequalities. This in turn will make them even more reliant on the assets and activities that contribute to pollution, trapping them in a vicious circle as carbon prices rise over time.

In order to address the social dimension of the climate transition, the EU established the Just Transition Mechanism. This is widely seen as an honest, albeit insufficient, attempt to address the social dimension by investing more money in some of Europe's energy-intensive and coal-mining regions and by helping them establish alternative development strategies. Since certain jobs are expected to be phased out and replaced by others, reskilling has assumed new importance.

In the EU policy domain, the European Skills Agenda has the task of identifying the key sectors that will be disrupted by the green and digital transitions and of working with relevant social partners to design upskilling and reskilling strategies. Nevertheless, social considerations should be embedded more structurally in all the EU's operations, starting with better monitoring of transformations and with knowledge-sharing about their causes and consequences. Consequently, the EU and its member states will need to invest more resources not only in the transition to a sustainable economy but also in improved understanding of the distributional outcomes of Green Deal measures at all policy levels.

Europe's fight for health and unity

COVID-19: A MEDICAL EMERGENCY

In March 2020, European countries were suddenly overwhelmed by the Covid-19 pandemic, originating from China. The unprecedented nature of this shock may explain why most national governments, together with the leaders of EU institutions, were slow and inconsistent in their responses to the emergency. At the same time, it was quickly understood that the challenge was to tackle each front of a threefold healthcare, economic and social crisis simultaneously. The search for the appropriate tools and strategies thus began.

What did the world know about the novel coronavirus – or the disease that resulted from it: Covid-19 – in March 2020? Not much, apart from the fact that it probably first spread from a market in the city of Wuhan in China, and that certain animals may have played an important part in transmitting it to humans. It was feared – and then soon confirmed by statistics – that the new coronavirus would be much more dangerous to life than the better-known influenza virus. It would spread faster and be five to six times more deadly.

As more and more people in Europe fell ill, and Covid-19 became the top issue in public discourse, our daily lives changed. More frequent hand washing was recommended to all, and hand-sanitizing liquids appeared in both public spaces and workplaces. People dropped the habit of shaking hands, occasionally replacing it with bumped fists or elbow contact. Kissing was discouraged, even in intimate relationships. Wearing face masks became increasingly common, and often mandatory in enclosed spaces.

While all such behavioural adjustments played an important part, the central element of the anti-Covid strategies of European governments has been the enforcement of social (or rather physical) distancing and the implementation of lockdowns, at least in the first phase, when bringing the spread of the virus under control required a bold and concerted effort. Rapid and comprehensive lockdowns paid off when implemented, while the failure to cancel major sporting events and mass rallies resulted in an explosion of the epidemic in Italy, Spain and the United Kingdom. Declining to prevent domestic travel among the population (from one side of the country to the other, or from urban to rural locations) was also an early policy failure, especially in France and Italy.

The emergency measures were inevitable to the extent that there was neither a vaccine to prevent Covid-19 infection, nor a treatment to cure it. Until effective vaccination became available and reached the critical mass of the population needed to develop herd immunity, society had to be prepared for more lockdowns. However, the forms taken by the various lockdowns differed depending on many factors, including the intensity of the pandemic, the resilience of healthcare systems, and economic as well as psychosocial considerations. Whether and precisely how to limit in-store shopping and to what extent standard schooling should be suspended represented major dilemmas for governments. When implementing emergency measures, governments had to factor in how prioritizing the fight against the coronavirus could result in a lack of adequate attention for other, more familiar diseases, as well as the consequences for mental health of lockdowns and other restrictions on daily life.

Since those who contracted the new coronavirus did not show symptoms for up to a week, the availability and intensity of testing became a strategic factor in the phase of taming the pandemic, and also in the subsequent phase of pushing it back. It was understood that eliminating the pandemic would require tremendous coordination and collective sacrifice, while eradicating the coronavirus completely would be practically impossible. According to the top US expert Anthony Fauci, 70–85% of the population would need to be vaccinated to reach herd immunity (or population immunity),[28]

---

28 Being sufficiently vaccinated originally meant having received two doses in most cases, which by the end of 2021 was increased to three doses (for the adult population).

a situation that comes about when a large portion of a community becomes immune to a given disease, making its spread from person to person unlikely and its symptoms mild.

In the spring of 2020, government policies and public expectations alike were aligned according to a model dubbed 'the hammer and the dance'. This model assumed that, in the first phase, when the pandemic caught societies and governments unprepared, infections would skyrocket and could only be pushed back by strictly enforced social distancing and lockdowns (the 'hammer'). This might be a relatively short period, perhaps only a matter of a few months; however, it would be followed by a much longer period during which the various restrictive measures would be gradually eased, only to be reinforced once more if the spread of the virus again accelerated (the 'dance'). The general assumption was that the scale of the problem would never return to the level experienced in the first phase. However, in the last quarter of 2020 we saw that this expectation was false, at least with respect to Europe and North America – and this initial misperception was not without consequences.

In other words, it was not only in the first phase of the crisis response that trial-and-error approaches were a widespread phenomenon, but also (and perhaps even more so) in the second half of 2020. Though it was understood that the countries that had effectively pushed back against Covid-19 (especially in East Asia, and in South Korea and Taiwan above all) had applied rigorous testing and contact tracing, this did not result in a universal best practice that could be copied and applied in other countries. Some countries in Europe (e.g. Slovakia) embarked on the comprehensive testing of their populations at certain points, but just like contact tracing this remained a matter of capacity and was subject to various other considerations.

The military was rolled out in various places to help with either logistics or with checks, and we also saw curfews of various types becoming part of the toolkit. Travel restrictions became widespread, with attempts at selectivity based on the presence of the coronavirus in various countries or regions of origin. In the second year of the pandemic, large sections of society started to tire of restrictive government measures, with or without being influenced by conspiracy theories or anti-vaccination ideologies. Anti-lockdown demonstrations became frequent, and the question of whether to make vaccination mandatory – or at least mandatory for certain age groups or certain professions – became a much more complex debate than had originally been envisaged by those following a purely medical rationale.

The best-known example of a failed experiment is the short-lived British strategy of herd immunity without vaccination, which became unpalatable as soon as it was understood that it was based on the calculable death rate among the older generation. The United Kingdom was not alone in this approach: it was also found in the Dutch and Swedish anti-Covid-19 policies, and in every other country where enforcement of the lockdown strategy was less strict. Sweden remained committed to a policy based on public trust that, by the end of 2020, had produced a higher level of fatality than in comparable European countries (although this still leaves open the question of the comparative assessment of different strategies in the long run). Herd immunity without mass vaccination was certainly not the only flawed approach that was tried: inconsistencies both great and small can be pointed out in many cases. For example, some governments attributed a great deal of importance to contact tracing (i.e. the process of identifying people who may have come into contact with someone already known to be infected) but without also introducing mass testing or adequate restrictions on mass gatherings and meetings.

As the medical emergency evolved, the focus of government actions also shifted. The first lockdown, in the spring of 2020, was essentially about saving healthcare systems by avoiding a sudden rise in coronavirus cases that would have been unmanageable for hospitals. The most horrifying situation was observed in March 2020 in (Northern) Italy, where doctors on the frontline had to decide who would receive treatment and who would not, giving those in the second group a lower chance of survival. Within a few months, the pandemic in Europe was tamed and healthcare capacities improved, allowing a new phase with fewer restrictions. Nevertheless, the virus returned after the summer holidays, and the 'dance' began afresh with a new round of restrictive measures.

The second lockdown cycle, however, in the last quarter of 2020, differed from the first. This time around it was not so much the healthcare system as the education system that was at stake, and especially in the case of primary education. Students had almost all switched to online teaching and learning in the spring of 2020, but this forced experiment was revealed to be less educationally effective than conventional schooling. Without any effort to (at least partly) restore standard forms of education, future generations would suffer greatly, and knowledge and skill inequalities would grow enormously. For a revival of education, and to allow parents the opportunity to focus on work, there would need to be sacrifices elsewhere. This required not only coordination but also public consultation.

From the very start of the pandemic, the EU has played a significant role in public discussions, as well as in the coordinated crisis response. The closure of intra-European borders was a reflexive reaction by governments, and the European Commission had to find the fastest route to reopening in order to minimize the damage to the deeply integrated European economy and to cross-border mobility, especially with respect to workers and students. Governments of member states also called on the EU to lead the tasks of vaccine development, procurement and distribution, not only to boost the speed of vaccination but also to ensure the even distribution of the available vaccines, and to thereby facilitate revitalization and economic recovery in Europe as a whole. The EU's role thus became increasingly important from the medical point of view, absolutely vital for the economy, and key determinant of the short- and long-term social impacts.

A JOINT RESPONSE TO THE JOBS CRISIS

The impact of the coronavirus crisis on economic growth was immediate and severe. Among OECD member countries, GDP dropped substantially in the first quarter of 2020, despite the fact that the governments of most OECD countries had put meaningful containment measures in place as early as the second half of March. The second quarter of 2020 saw a dramatic fall in all OECD countries, without exception: on average, GDP was expected to fall by 13.2% across OECD countries, exceeding the rate of decline at the time of the 2009 Great Recession. The drop in GDP was expected to be particularly severe in Spain and the United Kingdom (–19%) but also in France and Ireland (–18%).

Some specific sectors, such as tourism, (long-haul) transportation, hospitality and entertainment, suffered massively in 2020, and these sectors contributed disproportionately to rising unemployment. On the other hand, digital products and services saw a rise in demand, meaning that the digital giants experienced further growth and rising profits as a result of Covid-19.

The need for certain types of economic activity to continue despite the health emergency gave rise to a new term: essential workers (or key workers). It also became increasingly apparent that a large portion of this essential work was performed by EU migrants (often from Romania and Bulgaria). When the pandemic started, these workers were initially sent back to their home countries, but owing to their indispensable contribution they were later brought back to their workplaces through special transfers, even when travel restrictions for most of the population were intensifying. Travel and working conditions for these workers became the focus of serious concern.

Once it was understood that a great deal of economic and social activity would have to stop in order to slow the spread of the novel coronavirus, public attention shifted to rapidly rising unemployment as one of the most serious risks.[29] Alongside national governments, the EU was expected not only to mobilize existing instruments but also to rapidly develop new ones. Within just a few weeks, the European Commission duly put forward a proposal for the creation of a 'European instrument for temporary support to mitigate unemployment risks in an emergency', known for short as SURE. The core idea of SURE is that, when a member state experiences a sudden severe increase in unemployment, and a consequent rise in planned and actual public expenditure due to the application of schemes aiming

---

29   The explosion of unemployment is best illustrated by the fact that in a single week in March 2020 there were more than 3 million new applicants for unemployment benefits in the United States. The US recession was particularly harsh on Americans of colour. By the end of 2021, the unemployment rate among black Americans stood at 7.1%, while it was only 3.2% among whites.

to preserve employment, it can request financial assistance under the new facility to cover a significant part of this additional expenditure. The types of expenditure considered relevant relate to the extension or creation of short-time work (STW) schemes or similar measures designed to protect workers from the risk of unemployment and the loss of income. SURE thus represents an incentive to apply the STW approach in order to combat the pandemic recession, and it also acts to discourage governments and businesses from allowing easy dismissals and a rapid rise in the number of the jobless.

From a financial point of view, SURE was launched as a scheme for loans from the EU to the member states, with the total loans available amounting to up to €100 billion.[30] SURE added not only a new budgetary tool to the EU's arsenal but also a new way of raising and providing resources. It did not require any upfront cash contributions from national governments; instead, to back the lending scheme, member states had to commit to 'irrevocable and callable' guarantees to the EU budget totalling €25 billion. Backed by EU member states, the system enjoys a high credit rating, enabling the European Commission to contract loans on the financial markets under the most favourable conditions, with the purpose of on-lending them to the given member state requesting financial assistance.

The SURE financial scheme was innovative, but STW solutions were not invented in 2020 by the EU: they had already been popularized through examples in Germany and some of its neighbours. In previous recessions, starting from the early 1990s, the reduction of weekly working time (i.e. internal flexibility) was increasingly used as an alternative to large-scale dismissals (i.e. external flexibility). By the time of the eurozone crisis, this was seen as the gold standard both economically and socially, without assuming that it would serve as a universal solution or any kind of silver bullet. STW arrangements (or, in German, *Kurzarbeit*) resulted in a fall

---

30   The legal basis proposed by the Commission is Articles 122(1) and 122(2) of the Treaty on the Functioning of the European Union (TFEU) (https://eur-lex. europa.eu/legal-content/EN/TXT/?uri=CELEX:12016E122). See D'Alfonso (2020).

in the productivity of labour but made it easier for firms to recover production after a recession, while also limiting crisis-driven social dislocation. Time spent not working was often used for organizing training for workers.

While a consensus evolved that the STW arrangement was a much better option than unemployment, it was also understood that this option is not available everywhere and that there are certain preconditions for it to work well. Based on the specific features of countries that have pioneered STW schemes, we can identify not only the merits but also the limitations of *Kurzarbeit*. It requires three main preconditions to work well: (1) the economic downturn should be caused by a demand-side shock, after which the same economic structure can bounce back; (2) there should be a strong partnership between employers and trade unions (facilitating tailor-made schemes for a company or industry);[31] and (3) there should be the financial capacity to provide support from either an unemployment fund or elsewhere. These preconditions cannot be found everywhere, due to diverse political and economic frameworks and institutional traditions. Consequently, an EU scheme focusing on *Kurzarbeit* risked being biased in favour of better-off workers in countries with stronger industrial relations, leaving less secure workers to rely on potentially inadequate benefit schemes in more precarious countries.

Limiting EU solidarity to only those workers whose jobs can be saved has also raised questions. During the recession triggered by Covid-19, the number of people unemployed was bound to rise, not just because of the likelihood of dismissal but also because in such circumstances some companies simply die. Besides, many people had temporary contracts from before the crisis, and in the emergency situation most of these were simply not renewed, which meant there were many who ended up unemployed without being dismissed either de facto or de jure. Most of those employees would be unlikely to be considered under STW schemes, and neither would

---

31   Focusing on the example of Austria, Schnetzer *et al.* (2020) stress the importance of social partners in negotiation, and the resulting effectiveness of STW arrangements during the Covid-19 crisis.

the self-employed. It was thus particularly important that the SURE initiative (together with various national job-saving and income support schemes) would be open to the self-employed. Even with these considerations, however, SURE remains an exclusive support tool.

The creation and successful roll-out of SURE did not eliminate the need for a European unemployment insurance or reinsurance scheme, which would represent ex ante solidarity and would function as automatically as possible. In a sense, SURE can be seen as a complement to 'normal' unemployment insurance: it adds 'job insurance' in the context of a specific temporary emergency created by a large-scale, exogenous disaster. So conceived, it might turn out to be a specific 'plug-in' to a genuine European unemployment insurance scheme, ready to be installed immediately in the context of exceptional emergencies.

A BUDGET REVOLUTION: SOLIDARITY REBORN

In two recent crises, the EU spectacularly failed to display coordination and solidarity. Firstly, with the eurozone debt crisis, a great many wrong policies were tried before the path of shared recovery was found in 2012. Then, in 2015, the refugee crisis exposed deep divisions that prevented the EU from acting forcefully to save lives and protect the dignity of migrants. The reputation of the EU suffered both internally and worldwide as a result.

In 2020 a significant – if not striking – contrast could be detected between the austerity-focused answer to the eurozone debt crisis in the early 2010s and the willingness to engage in countercyclical policies, and in job and income protection, during the coronavirus-driven recession. This time around, it was not only progressives but also most liberals and conservatives who adopted or advocated Keynesian policies. Fiscal restrictions, as well as competition rules, were rapidly sidelined. The rise of public debt as a result of Covid-19 was a given, making the somewhat controversial modern monetary theory (MMT) the intellectual winner of the day. But even outside the cult of MMT, it had to be recognized that public investment had simply suffered too much in the previous (neoliberal) decades, and that a major correction was needed.

Suddenly, what Richard Nixon said fifty years earlier became true: 'we are all Keynesians now' (even if this was a kind of emergency Keynesianism, in many cases one without conviction). But allowing public deficits to grow well beyond standard ceilings was not the only policy: practically all European governments also introduced STW schemes, wage subsidies, new income protection schemes, or a combination thereof. Although these schemes varied greatly in terms of generosity, in most cases they had to be extended well into 2021.

In the language of economists, it is technically correct to say that the pandemic is a 'symmetrical crisis', but in the imbalanced context of Economic and Monetary Union, it was possible that the coronavirus-driven recession would lead to hugely asymmetric consequences, further increasing the vicious (path-dependent) polarization between north and south. The understanding of this risk resulted in the rapid curtailment of some nasty spats in the Eurogroup, and by May 2020 there could already be seen a deep shift in attitudes that, if sustained through the coming years, could turn out to be a game changer not only for short-term economic recovery but also for the longer-term reconstruction of the EU.

During a record-breaking 100-hour meeting in July 2020, the European Council decided to create an effective EU-level fiscal capacity to counteract the recession that had been triggered by the Covid-19 pandemic. The main elements of this are the newly conceived crisis fund (Next Generation EU, or NGEU)[32] and the seven-year EU budget (the Multiannual Financial Framework, or MFF), to which NGEU is attached. In terms of size, the most significant component of the package is the Recovery and Resilience Facility (RRF), which consists of large-scale financial support (up to €310 billion in grants and up to €250 billion in loans) to support both public investments and reforms, focusing on green and digital transformations.

At the same time, a breakthrough in one area does not necessarily signal progress everywhere. Quite the contrary: sometimes there is a price to be paid for a critical advance, and we saw an example of that here. The European Council was about to include a decision on a serious and effective rule-of-law mechanism as part

---

32   URL: https://bit.ly/3uTxq8S.

of the MFF deal, but eventually the adopted language did not go beyond the usual generalities. The main reason for this was the continuing inability of the European People's Party to sort out its internal divisions on this issue, with a secondary reason being the decision by the so-called Frugal Four (the Netherlands, Austria, Sweden and Denmark, later followed by Finland to make it the Frugal Five) to misuse their political capital and, instead of focusing on improving the functioning of the EU budget, seeking to achieve symbolic victories. While their priorities could be portrayed as prudent and a democratic representation of taxpayers' interests, the frugal group did cause significant damage to the EU budget, and thus to the spirit of community and solidarity. Instead of using the post-Brexit moment as an opportunity to bury the poisonous practice of rebates, they sought to increase them even further. In the conventional budget (the MFF) they weakened the tools that represent a clear European added value in resource allocation (e.g. Erasmus, Just Transition). And in the new budget component (the NGEU) they insisted on reducing the allocation for transfers in favour of the allocation for loans, making it somewhat less effective in helping the regions that had suffered most from the pandemic recession. The new budget package was eventually adopted at the end of 2020, after the European Council and the European Parliament had agreed on all the pieces of the puzzle. However, given the deeper-than-expected recession and the stubborn divergence within the eurozone, experts soon expressed doubt over whether the funds would be sufficient to counteract the risk of economic and social polarization (see Heimberger 2021).

It cannot be stressed enough that the repositioning of Germany in the European debate has been a precondition for a new fiscal approach to emerge at the EU level. Chancellor Angela Merkel, who had already brought about major U-turns in German domestic politics (on family policy, nuclear energy and immigration), then orchestrated another reorientation that has extraordinary significance for the survival of the EU. The fact that Germany, thanks to SPD politicians and intellectuals, has shifted away from its own legacy of frugality made it possible for Berlin to be driver of this decision-making process.

In May 2020, one week before the Commission's MFF proposal was due to be put forward, Merkel publicly aligned herself with French President Emmanuel Macron's position on economic governance, despite France having failed to receive an adequate response from Germany over the previous years (following Macron's 2017 speech at the Sorbonne). Ironically, the controversial decision of the German Constitutional Court on ECB competences contributed to the shift of position in Berlin by setting limits on ECB action and, perhaps unintentionally, prompting fiscal policy into action so as to avoid the risks of over-reliance on the ECB. The German presidency of the Council of the European Union in the second half of 2020 was an additional (highly favourable) circumstance that facilitated the necessary political decisions.[33]

In spring 2020 the Covid-19 crisis showed that the minimalist approach to the EU's role in emergency management was not sustainable. The issue was not only ex post solidarity coordination but also the establishment of greater safety and stabilization mechanisms, including in public finance. Consequently, the German presidency had to not simply broker a new budget for the EU but also create a consensus over that reinvented budget – and all within a few weeks. This is the area where the Covid-19 crisis triggered the most profound paradigm shift for Europe – one that could even be described as a Copernican revolution in EU public finance.

Besides fiscal affairs, it is also worth mentioning the social dimension of the German presidency. The coalition government was preparing for Council conclusions that would endorse EU-level minimum standards for national minimum wages, but their ambition went beyond the question of minimum wages and extended to minimum income schemes. More precisely, Germany wanted to see EU-level minimum standards for minimum income protection schemes in order to protect people from poverty and social exclusion across the EU, and to thereby facilitate labour market inclusion and serve as an economic stabilizer in times of crisis. In the current

---

33 The German coalition government took over the rotating presidency of the Council of the European Union on the 1st of July, at a critical time that even without the Covid-19 crisis would have been a decisive juncture.

circumstances, the importance of minimum income schemes is also highlighted by the need to combat the socio-economic consequences of the Covid-19 pandemic. Overall, the German presidency of the Council helped to make significant steps forward in the social dimension, while also helping to prepare the ground for the ambitious Portuguese presidency.

Though widely celebrated in July 2020, the EU's new fiscal package was not a done deal until December. In the interim, the EU's seven-year financial framework (the MFF) and its recovery budget (the NGEU) were held hostage by a bitter dispute over the rule of law. The European Parliament established itself as a guardian of EU values, imposing its requirements at least on the spending machinery of the Union. Following the July meeting of the European Council, the German presidency began working on a solution that the majority of MEPs considered to be too unambitious to deal effectively with some rogue governments in the east. However, once the Parliament ensured that the mechanism would be equipped with real teeth, the two governments most affected – those of Hungary and Poland – expressed their readiness to veto the fiscal package altogether. Despite this, it became clear that the Parliament's position was indeed rooted in popular support, with more than three-quarters of European citizens wanting to see a connection between rule-of-law requirements and EU spending, including the more than seven out of ten Hungarians who agreed with this conditionality.[34]

Of the two countries in focus, Hungary in particular infuriated the democratic-minded majority in 2020, since it was all too obvious from the very start of the spring lockdown that Prime Minister Viktor Orbán would use the medical emergency as another opportunity for a personal power grab, as well as for a broad-daylight asset grab for his entourage. The Polish government, on the other hand, faced a series of street demonstrations against their overreach on reproductive rights, while also experiencing some instability within their ruling coalition. The stand-off ended with an agreement on the conditionality mechanism that followed the demands of the European

---

34 URL: www.euractiv.com/section/justice-home-affairs/news/european-citizen s-support-linking-eu-funds-to-rule-of-law-survey-shows.

Parliament, while at the same time allowing for some delay in implementation (due to the need for legal checks by the Court of Justice and for an outline of the procedural details by the Commission). The rule-of-law stand-off demonstrated that European institutions can achieve what they want and will not blink in any political poker game when giving in would pose a high risk to the integrity of the EU.

Altogether, the creation of NGEU as a strategic tool of the pandemic crisis response was more than just an example of a proverbial step in the right direction.[35] The newly created instruments appear to have some very important features that had the potential to stop the MFF standing on its head and to place it upon its feet (to borrow an expression from German philosophy), by assuming a proper stabilization role at the Union level. In addition to various forms of passive support (e.g. suspending fiscal or competition rules in times of crisis), the EU has now been equipped with new instruments to provide active support. With NGEU, a new type of fiscal capacity has emerged, and this was only possible by breaking some taboos. Firstly, the 1% glass ceiling was broken, since the combined share of the new instruments compared with total EU gross national income now amounts to 1.8%. Secondly, EU countries will borrow jointly under the NGEU, and will do so for the sake of countercyclical stabilization. And thirdly, although we might have heard a thousand times in the past decade that the EU is not a 'transfer union', cross-border transfers have now started to be implemented from borrowed resources (to be repaid by 2058). These new features have naturally also opened up a new debate over making NGEU a permanent instrument rather than a temporary one.

SAVING COHESION POLICY

Although not directly addressed by the framework of the Social Pillar, one egregious and critical manifestation of inequalities within the EU is that witnessed at the regional level. Cohesion – the EU policy

---

35   As a strategic tool, NGEU potentially offers a template to respond to subsequent crises and shocks, starting with the 2022 war in Ukraine.

designed to address this issue – receives far less attention than it merits, with its future being called into question on every occasion when elaboration of the EU's seven-year budget features on the agenda. According to Dauderstädt and Keltek (2017), regional inequalities and their significance are routinely underestimated both in statistics and by government players. Their calculations show that pan-European inequality decreased in the period between EU enlargement and the crisis of 2009, before increasing temporarily thereafter. It has since decreased again, albeit at a much slower pace than before the Great Recession. In general, however, the post-2004 eastward enlargement (mainly through the accession of Romania and Bulgaria in 2007) has greatly exacerbated inequalities among the populations of the EU, and many underestimate the significance of this fact. Progress in this area will require a much more resolute strategy if we do not wish to risk disintegration of the single market.

In the early 1990s, Jacques Delors very consciously supplemented the newly created single market with a reformed and strengthened cohesion policy. However, the subsequent eastward enlargement and profound economic crises put this EU policy to the test. In the debates over the MFF initiated by the Juncker Commission, cohesion occupied a defensive position from the outset, branded as an 'old' policy and thus doomed, in a top-down budgeting process, to lose out to 'newer' community needs (such as expenditures related to migration or external affairs).

If one area of consensus on EU integration does exist, then it is the single market, which is nevertheless unsustainable in the long term without devoting community funds to supporting the advancement of lower-income participants (those 'lagging behind the competition'). By no means is it written in the stars that cohesion policy should disappear or even be scaled back. If the EU contains a more heterogeneous mix of countries and regions than before – several of them with incomes well below average[36] – then few logical arguments

---

36 The Commission's cohesion report of April 2017 revealed that one-sixth of the EU's population live in regions where the average income does not reach half of the EU average. These regions are located mainly on the southern and eastern peripheries.

can be raised in favour of the depletion of cohesion instruments. Even so, the grave danger of this happening did enter the conversation during the MFF debates of 2018–19, due chiefly to, on the one hand, misconstruing the consequences of Brexit and, on the other, the prevalence of anti-EU attitudes in some beneficiary countries.

It may sound absurd, but during the MFF negotiations in the shadow of Brexit many countries – principally among the net contributors – claimed that the departure of the British meant there would simply be insufficient funds for some of the bigger items of expenditure (such as agricultural policy and cohesion). These warnings failed to take into account not only that the United Kingdom was one of the higher-income countries within the EU but also – and most crucially – that the British enjoyed the first and by far the largest budgetary rebate. Elimination of the system of illogically granted rebates might in itself have halved the loss of revenue caused by Britain's departure. (It is a different matter that other net contributors insisted on keeping it, so that in the end it has remained in place.)

However, a problem arose that was still more serious than these superficial calculations; namely, that in Hungary and Poland – despite a largely pro-EU climate of public opinion – anti-Brussels sentiment and the sabotaging of common solutions (and subsequently of EU law) became the guiding motives of government behaviour in a variety of areas. The Hungarian government was taking no small risk in inciting Brussels-phobia. After a decade and a half of EU membership, everyone in Hungary had come to recognize the indispensable role played by EU funding in investments affecting almost every branch of the economy. At the same time, a certain amount of experience had also been accumulated about the weaknesses of this policy, and how to abuse EU subsidies.

There are member countries both old and new that commit significant errors in the use of EU funds from time to time – and if an instrument is not functioning well, it becomes harder to argue in favour of maintaining it. Other countries might want serial abusers to explain why they have asked for money when they have proven unable to properly use the funds granted them so far. Hungary counts as an extreme example among the twenty-seven member countries, since here the diversion of EU funds for party political purposes is blatant.[37] In this autocratic system, cohesion policy serves to maintain an 'industry' whose participants have specialized in services connected to managing the 'distribution of cash'. In many cases, rather than structural funds being used to finance existing development activity, more or less meaningful projects have been cooked up to match the prospective available resources. Expectations of partnership or social consultation have largely remained theoretical.

Cohesion policy can only be renewed and secured in the long term if the affected regions themselves come forward with viable proposals for their accelerated development, e.g. with respect to the use of EU funds. As for ensuring that funds are deployed in accordance with the rules, an important innovation of recent years is the establishment of a public prosecutor's office watching over EU funds, which has stronger powers to proceed against fraudsters and profiteers than the current European Anti-Fraud Office (OLAF). Although this new creation is not a bad idea, it remains voluntary without amendment of the Treaty, and unsurprisingly Hungary and Poland have no wish to join.

Another opportunity for reform might come via transformation of the institutional system that controls the use of funds. Temptation is the first step along the road to abuse, and temptation may arise because the EU's money is handled not by EU institutions but by the member states themselves. The Commission's role in planning is limited, while supervision is indirect and subject to delays in implementation. It can happen that the EU will seek to reclaim money going back 6–8 years because of irregularities. To prevent this, the competent office of the European Commission (specifically, the relevant directorate-general) may interrupt payments or suspend programmes if it is not absolutely convinced of their regularity. This leads to delays and may result in a 'financial correction', although the member state is generally able to reprogramme the withdrawn amount. This situation would be improved if the European

---

37 Those interested in the functioning of cohesion in Hungary might leaf through a study prepared by KPMG and GKI or a lengthy analysis by the Budapest Institute. Besides the macroeconomic impacts, these studies summarize many experiences at the micro level, also drawing institutional conclusions that may prove useful in debates and discussions of possible solutions at the EU level.

Commission, and not the individual member country, were to invite tenders for the amount withdrawn in the case of a correction, or for funds that remains unused beyond a deadline because of delays. Most of the funds would remain in the hands of the member country, but greater attention would be paid to ensuring those funds did not slip out of control. Such a reform would require the EU to take on more staff, but the investment would certainly pay off, not only financially but also by strengthening confidence in the EU.

It is also important that cohesion should not be a 'policy for the poor' (either now or in future). The British example is a case in point, as while both Conservative and Labour governments bargained well in Brussels, the financial benefits of membership were concentrated in London and Southern England. Successive British governments did not adequately tackle the issue of regional cohesion, failing to support disadvantaged regions, such as in Northern England. In many instances, subsidized regions such as Wales were insufficiently aware that their well-being was in large part due to subsidies, and that these came from the EU budget.

All this must naturally be borne in mind when shaping cohesion policy in future. Internal polarization can have a destructive effect in richer countries as well. Cohesion policy cannot be taken away from the more developed member states, but neither can governments be left to forget about certain disadvantaged regions. This signals a need for a greater degree of conditionality and stronger EU engagement in the planning and execution of development programmes. Greater conditionality may be the solution to the problem of economic convergence not necessarily going hand in hand with social development in converging countries. If, however, the Social Pillar remains entirely optional and is not linked to cohesion, this will essentially mean that we have accepted that the fruits of economic growth may only be harvested by a narrow stratum of society.

Beneficiary countries also need to realize that the EU's social policy initiatives are intended to help achieve economic and social policy goals alike. Harmony, not tension, needs to be created between the two. It is also necessary to reinforce the idea that cohesion policy (including the operation of structural funds) is an inalienable part of the EU's single market. Lastly, every period of planning must present concrete proposals to improve the quality of EU regulation. Such proposals are of course only credible if they rely on objective analysis and evaluation independent of government.

The strategy of beneficiary countries has traditionally been to pursue active engagement among the 'Friends of Cohesion',[38] which, though important, is not enough. On the one hand, there must be less abuse (or suspicion of abuse) surrounding EU funds. As for the insufficiency of funding, one direction of change has been the broadening of the role of combined financial instruments,[39] which may result in both the expansion of funds and the enhancement of transparency. By coupling the resources of development banks with EU funds, we build a bridge for those who, with time, will no longer need non-refundable support, but who may thus gain experience in the area of bank financing.

The EU has provided the countries that joined in 2004 and after with a chance to achieve long-term economic convergence. For us to speak of genuine convergence, however, a number of instruments may require a substantial redesign. One such redesign would involve a more tightly woven relationship between cohesion policy and the Social Pillar.

ACTION FOR EQUAL SOCIAL RIGHTS

As the pandemic surged from one wave to the next, EU actors were keen to demonstrate that launching SURE was not the last step in strengthening the social dimension in the face of multiple adversities, it was simply the first. A demonstration of the EU's adherence to the original ambition expressed in the 2017 European Pillar of Social Rights took place in spring 2021 through discussions in the

---

38 This group consists of Bulgaria, Croatia, Cyprus, the Czech Republic, Estonia, Greece, Hungary, Italy, Latvia, Lithuania, Malta, Poland, Portugal, Romania, Slovakia, Slovenia and Spain.

39 These innovations were launched within the European Regional Development Fund (ERDF), but they also inspired the administrators of the European Social Fund (ESF) by opening up the opportunity for microloan schemes and local governments to issue bonds for the financing of social policy programmes.

field of social policy, culminating in an informal summit in Porto, Portugal, on 7–8 May. Twenty-four of the twenty-seven EU presidents and prime ministers participated. Ahead of Porto, the European Commission put forward an action plan aimed at effective implementation of the pillar (the European Pillar of Social Rights (EPSR) Action Plan) to ensure that participants would discuss not simply general principles and aspirations but concrete initiatives and practical steps.

The EPSR Action Plan was meant to be a response to the demand created and sustained by the social policy community after the proclamation of the Social Pillar, which was deliberately produced as a declarative and somewhat theoretical document without the intention on the part of the Juncker Commission to follow it up in practice within the time frame available to them. In addition, the creation of the EPSR Action Plan was further encouraged by fresh Eurobarometer findings that revealed that nearly nine in ten Europeans (88%) regard a 'social Europe' as important to them personally, while more than seven in ten (71%) believe that the lack of social rights is currently a serious problem (Eurobarometer 2020).

Beyond displaying a long list of EU activities in the fields of employment policy, social policy and equal opportunities, the EPSR Action Plan – released on 3 March 2021 – proposed three headline targets in order to better monitor progress towards the goals set out in the Social Pillar. The first of these proposed that the employment rate among those aged 20–64 be increased to 78%, from 72.5% in 2020. In line with this, the gender employment gap should be halved, and the share of young people not in employment, education or training (NEETs) should be reduced to 9%, from 12.6% in 2019. The new targets would need to be reached by 2030.

Interestingly, two-thirds of the actions listed in the EPSR Action Plan had first been proposed in either 2020 or during the first quarter of 2021, i.e. prior to the Porto summit. In other words, the role of the Porto summit was not to launch fresh thinking or open up new initiatives but rather to gather political support for policies that had already been put forward by the von der Leyen Commission as far back as its inception. On the other hand, with the passing of the Porto summit and the Portuguese presidency, the notion that everything 'social' is for the member states to take care of started to return to EU-related discourse, not least because of the completely different priorities dominating the agenda of Slovenia's Council presidency, next in rotation after Portugal's. Adding to the ambivalence, Commission President Ursula von der Leyen did not consider the EPSR Action Plan important enough to mention in her State of the Union address in September 2021. Representing the social dimension in her speech was a minor youth mobility scheme called ALMA.[40] Observers might have therefore been left with the impression that social policy is a seasonal matter for Brussels.

On the other hand, for some aspects of the social agenda the von der Leyen Commission was visibly determined to reject the status quo and leave a durable legacy. Gender equality is one example. The European Commission that entered office in 2019 is the first in history to be headed by a female politician. The former German minister also wanted to ensure that the privilege would not be hers alone and that the entire Commission would shift towards a better gender balance. The aim to have a perfect balance between men and women at the top level of the Commission was nearly achieved in 2019, and subsequently the lower levels of the hierarchy were also impelled to make a proper effort to promote female officials to positions as directors and heads of units.

Perhaps even more important is what the Commission has started to do to improve the social situation of millions of European women. Equality Commissioner Helena Dalli has promoted binding pay-transparency legislation to help close a gender pay gap that sees women paid an average of 14.1% less than men across the

---

40 ALMA (Aim, Learn, Master, Achieve) is a programme to help young people find their way on the job market, especially the most disadvantaged NEETs aged 18–30 who are vulnerable with respect to their chances of accessing work or training for specific reasons such as disability, long-term unemployment, insufficient school performance or vocational skills, or migration background. ALMA offers participants (1) a supervised stay abroad for a period of 2–6 months in another EU member state and (2) a comprehensive project cycle involving coaching and counselling at every step. As well as creating new connections across Europe, the ultimate aim of ALMA is to better integrate young people into society and to help them find their place in the job market by providing opportunities to improve skills, knowledge and experience.

twenty-seven EU member states.[41] Under this legislation, employers may be prevented from quizzing job candidates on their current earnings because of new EU rules that aim to help women secure higher pay. If such questioning were to happen, it would count as a form of discrimination that the given candidate could report, since previous pay should have no bearing on the assessment of the applicant's skills and working abilities. On the other hand, candidates should have the right to ask prospective employers for pay information. Exposure of pay information is expected to help women judge if they are being paid fairly for the same work done by men, and it may help equality advocates and trade unions seek compensation for pay discrimination.

The proposed EU directive requires governments to set penalties, including fines, at a level they think will be effective if companies fail to supply information on potential pay gaps. Large firms with more than 250 employees would be obliged to publish information on pay for female and male workers and to supply more detailed information to their staff. Smaller firms, which are often treated more lightly in EU legislation, would be required to supply pay information at a worker's request. These new rules are supposed to cover basic salaries, bonuses, overtime pay, pensions and expenses such as travel and housing allowances. However, the proposal does not demand that women be paid the same as men: it instead requires that any pay differences be based on clear criteria.

Needless to say, EU rules on pay transparency can only be small steps in a wider effort to close the pay gap and the even greater pension gap (30% on average in Europe). Gaps also exist in terms of participation and promotion, which partly explains the consequences for salaries and pensions. In the EU today, only 7% of CEOs are female, with women filling just 17% of all executive posts. In addition, female managers earn €10 per hour less than men. It

---

41   Evidence that publishing pay-related information has a positive impact on the capacity of women to negotiate higher wages has been observed in Sweden, Austria, Denmark and Finland, which all systematically gather data on gender pay differences. The UK regulations require companies with at least 250 employees to disclose the difference between men's and women's mean pay.

should also be noted that, despite a modest reduction in the gender pay gap being observed in some member states during the decade of the Europe 2020 Strategy, the pay gap typically increased in eastern EU countries (Slovenia, Poland, Hungary, Croatia, Lithuania and Latvia) as well as in Malta. This may be connected with a trend of large numbers of previously inactive women joining the labour force, which typically happened in job categories with low salaries.

During the pandemic period, a variety of studies looked into the effects of Covid-19 from the point of view of intergenerational and gender balances. It was quickly established that Covid-19's potential to be a life-threatening virus was particularly dangerous for the older generation. Though younger men and women can also fall victim to Covid-19, this occurs mainly if there is an underlying health condition, e.g. diabetes or obesity. The harm to young people tends to be more indirect (e.g. through interruptions to education and reductions in parents' incomes). Regarding the gender balance, significantly more men than women fell victim to Covid-19. But again, the burden on women – especially those working in the health and care sectors – grew disproportionately as a result of the healthcare emergency and the broader effects of the pandemic.

For progressive governments, the Covid-19 health crisis and the resulting economic recession provided an opportunity to demonstrate their added value, and indeed this opportunity was widely utilized, especially in the cases of Finland, Denmark and New Zealand. Sensitivity to the gender aspects of the crisis was one of the most important features of this impressive display. The key was to emphasize policies that ensured that the most vulnerable members of society would have a safety net to rely on during the crisis, and that the restart of the economy would be carried out with greater social equality and with improved income distribution patterns.[42]

---

42 One of the four pillars of the recovery and resilience plan in Spain, overseen by Deputy Prime Minister Nadia Calviño, was built around gender equality.

TOWARDS A HEALTH UNION

With the escalation of EU action during the maelstrom of the coronavirus pandemic, the idea of a European health union started to gain traction. This concept had already cropped up before Covid-19, but the pandemic made it compelling impossible to ignore. This was reflected in Commission President Ursula von der Leyen's first State of the Union speech, delivered in September 2020, in which she took the opportunity to thank all of Europe's frontline workers and gave a positive response to the July decision of the European Parliament regarding the creation of a health union. Considering that until recently those who wanted to shrink Brussels bureaucracy had routinely pointed to the health portfolio as the one to be culled in the absence of real EU competences, the health union now became a territory of real breakthrough.

Of course, a health union would not mean the EU would take over healthcare services or health insurance within its member states. However, a shared health response mechanism could make a difference in the case of future shocks, and a strengthened joint procurement mechanism would result in significant economies of scale. Minimum standards for healthcare enshrined in a directive would help prevent European healthcare from breaking up into first-class and second-class (and possibly third- and fourth-class) services, while the stress testing of national healthcare systems could help spot weaknesses that require reform and investment if those systems are to deliver according to citizens' expectations.

The setting of minimum standards and the introduction of stress testing also needs to reflect the fact that the eastern enlargement of the EU, together with some of the asymmetric recessions of the past two decades, triggered a large-scale migration of medical staff – including doctors as well as nurses – from the east towards the west and the north. Without a serious attempt to rebalance that also includes a material support component, these tendencies could cause irreversible damage to capacities in the countries of origin, and through this they could also contribute to more general Eurosceptic sentiment.

The European Health Emergency Preparedness and Response Authority (HERA) is envisaged as the core of any future European health union. Intended to be endowed with €50 billion, HERA would be a central element in strengthening the health union with better EU preparedness for and responses to serious cross-border health threats by enabling the rapid availability of, access to and distribution of the needed countermeasures. In addition, von der Leyen has proposed a European version of BARDA in order to drive biomedical innovation.[43] A vision for a healthier EU has also been outlined (EU4Health, covering 2021–7), with ambitious components that include a joint plan to beat cancer in Europe and an EU pharmaceutical strategy.

In her second State of the Union address, in September 2021, von der Leyen focused on what she considered proof of competent leadership: the fight against the Covid-19 pandemic and its consequences. This was all the more important since 2020 did not end well for the Commission in this regard. Once mass production of Covid vaccines began, the United Kingdom jumped ahead of the EU with delivery to its population, exposing weaknesses on the part of the Commission in dealing with such vital procurement procedures. On top of this, Russia brought out its Sputnik vaccine as early as EU-based producers did theirs, calling into question the supposed significant advantage of western biological and medical sciences. Before the European Parliament's plenary session, the Commission president nevertheless declared that the EU had successfully mastered the crisis (especially in comparison with the rest of the world), with more than 70% of the EU population vaccinated. Von der Leyen also noted that the EU's recovery fund (the RRF), which was adopted in December 2020, was being implemented.

Without doubt, the EU's measures to overcome the crisis bore fruit in the second year of the pandemic. Assuming a new coordinating role, the European Commission aimed to ensure that all member states received vaccines based on a fair distribution principle and that the roll-out began simultaneously across Europe. The overall picture improved as the year progressed from winter to summer, and the

---

43   The Biomedical Advanced Research and Development Authority (BARDA) is a US agency founded in 2006. It is now seen by EU officials as a model to be followed.

EU highlighted the benefits of joint procurement and distribution. However, what received less attention than it deserved was the slower progress with vaccination (and the higher Covid-related death rates) in some peripheral countries – especially in eastern member states – due to weaknesses in national health systems (linked to shortages of staff in particular).

Having said this, pushing back against 'vaccine nationalism' worked better within the EU than it did globally. The danger of uneven global distribution was highlighted by many, including Pope Francis. In his 2020 Christmas message, the pontiff opined that political and business leaders must not allow market forces and patent laws to take priority over making Covid-19 vaccines available to all, and he condemned nationalism and 'the virus of radical individualism'. EU High Representative Josep Borrell also outlined a vision for an international coordination role, according to which vaccines must be treated as a global public good and distributed based on medical need.

What happened in 2020–21 demonstrates that healthcare and public education are central parts of our civilization – or, as some would prefer to call it, our 'European way of life'. Hence, it is not primarily overall consumption levels that will have to be restored after the pandemic but the systems that support our social cohesion and enlightened values, with equality at the centre. EU institutions, now committed to promoting the European way of life, must play a role in forging a consensus around this strategy.[44] European coordination can help establish policies and practices – together with shared minimum standards – across a diverse community of countries. In this way the legitimacy of crisis response measures can be strengthened, both improving our chances of surviving pandemics and preserving our European civilization.

---

44   After some controversy in the autumn of 2019, the European Commission established a portfolio for 'Promoting our European way of life'. The controversy arose because originally the European way of life was to be 'protected', a thinly veiled meaning of which was protecting it primarily from the effects of migration.

Conclusion: the social union imperative

Following the 2019 European Parliament elections, and at the peak of the pandemic period, the institutions of the European Union launched the Conference on the Future of Europe (CoFoE) in order to engage in a dialogue with citizens and to collaboratively outline future options for integration. With its focus on the opportunity to engage with citizens, the CoFoE was primarily meant to address the EU's much-talked-about democratic deficit; at the same time, however, the Union must also contend with a much-less-talked-about social deficit. The global financial crisis and the eurozone crisis deepened both of these deficits, and the jury is still out as to whether further damage can be limited in the wake of the coronavirus pandemic.

Irrespective of the outcomes of the CoFoE, a different EU is already emerging from the Covid-19 maelstrom. Firstly, in relation to the EU budget, a new type of fiscal capacity has appeared. This was only possible by breaking some taboos. The 1% glass ceiling limiting the size of EU fiscal capacity has been broken, since the combined share of the new instruments compared with total EU gross national income now amounts to 1.8%. Secondly, EU countries will borrow jointly for the sake of countercyclical stabilization. And thirdly, although the mantra heard over the past decade is that the EU is not a 'transfer union', cross-country transfers are now set to be implemented from borrowed resources (to be repaid by 2058).

We saw that the EU performed better in 2020 than in the previous crises because it immediately connected the economic crisis response with a social agenda. However, what remains in question is not only short-term relief but the longer-term trajectory of the post-Covid era. The efforts to orchestrate recovery and reconstruction strategies show that the EU can find a way back to the spirit of 'smart, sustainable and inclusive growth'. For this to happen, however, EU policy coordination must ensure that the environmental and social commitments outlined before the crisis will be reinforced in this new era and not left to fall by the wayside. The 2017 Social Pillar, the 2021 EPSR Action Plan and the Porto summit have all energized debate around the notion of a social Europe, reassuring the stakeholder community and also raising expectations. The CoFoE should not be the last opportunity to express aspirations and policy proposals for strengthening the social dimension of the EU.

The book that best captures the spirit of the time is probably Colin Crouch's *Social Europe: A Manifesto*. Crouch does not simply offer a conventional argument for a social Europe. (Some totemic issues of the social policy debate in the European Parliament, such as the posting of workers, are completely absent from his book.) Instead, Crouch outlines his vision for nothing less than a social union, with due reference to Frank Vandenbroucke and Anton Hemerijck, who pioneered this concept (together with Maurizio Ferrera and others). He invokes Karl Polanyi to underpin the suggestion that 'moves to extend markets need to be accompanied by moves in social policy' (Crouch 2020, p. 47). He also integrates actions combating environmental damage and climate change into his vision of a social union, together with measures necessary to tackle the challenges of the digital transformation.

From the perspective of Crouch, Ferrera, Vandenbroucke or Hemerijck, the social union represents a qualitative leap beyond a conception of the EU in which social policy is an appendix to the main body of economic integration and governance. As Vandenbroucke very significantly underlines, 'a European Social Union is not a European Welfare State: it is a union of national welfare states, with different historical legacies and institutions'. However, since the functioning of the EU – and of economic governance in particular – has massive consequences for national industrial relations and welfare systems, mainly through their fiscal bases, there is a need for the safety nets of the individual member states to in turn be supported by an EU safety net.

In recent years, without any push in a federalist direction, the EU moved towards a banking union, a capital markets union, an energy union and even a security union. Subsequently, the Covid pandemic made the idea of a health union unavoidable. However, as Vandenbroucke argues, the health union must be part and parcel of a social union, given the centrality within all national welfare models in Europe of the right of equal access to health services. If the idea of a social union is rejected with simplistic references to subsidiarity, then the gap between the economic and social sides of integration will only widen further, and the legitimacy of EU integration will suffer.

It should not be overlooked that the arithmetic of EU politics has become more favourable for a strengthening of the social dimension, as Brexit signified the departure of the country that was least committed to the EU's social dimension. In previous years, British governments had used every opportunity to block the creation of a more social Europe. During the 2015–16 endgame, the Brexit referendum was fuelled by antipathy towards cross-border migration. However, the long-term project of taking the United Kingdom out of the EU reflected a rejection of the social market model that had become established on the continent. The decision of the continent's leaders not to bend before the demands of Britain (or, to be more precise, of England) strengthened their understanding of the role that social standards play in EU integration.

The lose–lose nature of Brexit left no doubt that economic damage would be suffered not only in the United Kingdom but also on the continent. On the other hand, losing the member that was most reluctant about European integration raised some hopes of a greater readiness to pull together and to deepen solidarity, and to relaunch the development of the EU's social dimension. Promising signs could already be seen under the Juncker Commission when the European Pillar of Social Rights was adopted as an EU-wide framework rather than one that would apply to the euro area only (the latter option was floated while there was still some optimism that the United Kingdom could remain in the EU).

The departure of the United Kingdom allows other countries to move much more freely towards deeper integration – if they wish to. Such an intention, however, cannot be taken for granted. In recent years, the reluctance of member states to deepen the social dimension of the EU has been attributed to a variety of factors. One factor relates to countries with high incomes and high social standards (e.g. Sweden and Austria), where a more social EU raises the fear of a downward adjustment of social standards. The second relates to opposition from politicians who consider social policy a threat to economic competitiveness (Orbán's Hungary in particular). Thirdly, there are countries that went through economic hardship and divergence (e.g. Spain and Italy) that may fear that enhanced EU social policy would bring greater conditionality and sanctions, when compliance with existing conditions has already been rather demanding. A fourth concern is that any further development of a social agenda would lead to a higher common budget, against which any Dutch government would be at the ready to assemble a politically colourful coalition.

An even greater geopolitical shock than Brexit hit Europe with Russia's unprovoked invasion of Ukraine in February 2022. At the time of writing, the trajectory of this brutal war cannot be judged, beyond the fact that the perpetrators of the war underestimated the determination of Ukrainians to resist, the capacity of the west to unite, and the possibility of popular support for the war within Russia unravelling. Suddenly, European governments and EU institutions had to focus on defence and security, raising concerns among climate policy and social policy stakeholders – as well as advocates of the rule of law – that these important policies and values, which had been prioritized on the EU agenda, would now be sidelined. There is no doubt that supporting the Ukrainian fight for independence through both aid and sanctions on Russia puts a burden on the shoulders of many Europeans, with decision-making often moving faster than the assessment of distributional effects. Even if EU countries themselves do not become directly involved in military conflict, a war in Eastern Europe can shift resources away from social policies and result in falling living standards. The severity of these effects depends on how quickly a balanced and sustainable peace arrangement between Russia and Ukraine can be negotiated – an arrangement that would probably entail a new and wide-reaching security architecture in Europe. At the same time, the shock of the war and the refugee influx it has triggered also gives rise to new forces of solidarity, and potentially to new examples of social policy innovation that point towards renewed efforts to foster cohesion.

Notwithstanding economic and geopolitical shocks, the past decade also revealed an unambiguous endeavour to repair the damage caused by financial crises and correct the flaws in the EU's architecture. For some this endeavour was prompted by the warnings (and, in times of crisis, the alarming trends) visible in social statistics, and for others it was prompted by the dangerous rise of populism and Euroscepticism, and the resulting high risk of the disintegration of the EU. This serves to highlight even more clearly that the development of social models has always been a matter of political choices. Policy options have always existed and will continue to exist.

Following the 2009 Great Recession and the subsequent euro area debt crisis, a new movement for a reinforced social dimension has been pushing the EU beyond the limits set down in the past. The specific discussion on EU-wide unemployment insurance (or reinsurance) first developed within an epistemic community of experts and then benefitted from a snowballing effect, involving more and more political actors (such as MEPs and ministers). The compelling argument for the introduction of EU-wide unemployment (re)insurance derives from the severe divergence generated by the malfunctioning of Economic and Monetary Union, especially in times of crisis. The case for countercyclical social stabilization at the EU level is now a touchstone for a materially meaningful EU social dimension.

Moving beyond the phase of producing theoretical documents (the most important of which were the Social Pillar and the associated reflection paper), EU institutions were well prepared during the Covid-19 pandemic crisis to deliver 'de facto solidarity', whether this was through a giant leap to greater budgetary capacity in the form of Next Generation EU or through SURE, which aims to promote – but also financially support – short-time work arrangements in order to counter the harmful labour-market effects of a recession. Neither of the new instruments will suffice, however, without the creation of an EU safety net for those whose jobs cannot be saved in a period of economic downturn. In fact, a well-designed unemployment reinsurance scheme could even turn out to be a critical piece of the puzzle as EU institutions and member states return to the inevitable reform of old (and outdated) fiscal rules.

A major lesson to be drawn from the transformations of the past decades is that the social question in Europe remains inseparable from the economic one. However, because of the frequent lack of alignment between economic policy and social policy, citizens and stakeholders in social Europe are often left with the impression that the EU is playing fast and loose with the social question.

Since the launch of the 2000 Lisbon Strategy, the EU has played a major role in promoting shared objectives and facilitating a common methodology in the social policy domain. At the same time, common goals and methodologies have helped develop common solutions, bringing into the convergence process the tools, as well as the institutions, of national social models. In the spirit of Lisbon, any twenty-first-century EU social agenda must address new issues such as the impact of digitalization and robotization on labour, especially with respect to the effects of technological change on working conditions and income inequality.

However, it will never be enough if EU social policy is simply cultivated as a specific policy field with its own particular experts and stakeholders. The crux of the matter is to reconcile the economics with our social policy objectives, and to monitor the social dimension of all EU policy areas and tools, from trade to competition. As Seikel (2021) succinctly puts it: 'The formula for strengthening the social dimension of the EU can be formulated as follows: social minimum standards plus a reconfiguration of the internal market and EMU in a way that is compatible with the pillars of the European Social Model.'

The critical question today is whether the EU can provide material support to its member states and regions in a systematic way in order to meet common social standards and achieve commonly agreed goals. This brings us to the most essential question regarding the concept of a social union: its material basis. A social union cannot just mean more EU-level legislation, because it cannot be built purely through increased policy coordination or budgetary instruments. All three arms of governance have to play a role, and with the appropriate coordination. The time has come for a new architecture that would join together the many components – both old and new – that a social union would require. In the words of Maurizio Ferrera

(2018), the European social union would represent 'a fully-fledged institutional counterpart' to EMU, and it can be built using many existing building blocks alongside some new ones.

Reports of the death of the European social model during and after recent crises were greatly exaggerated. Nevertheless, it is also true that the eurozone crisis called into question whether the original model of EMU can be reconciled with democratic procedures within member states, and whether it represents a mortal threat to welfare states on the eurozone periphery. Debate over these problems has been extremely protracted, not least because social integration in Europe has always followed economic integration with a delay and on a much weaker legal footing. The gap has widened again, which also contributes to the decline of confidence in the EU in times of crisis.

For many, the Social Pillar represents hope. It may turn out to be the game changer that is needed to launch a round of actions addressing the social deficit. If its components are well designed and work together in concert, the move to a social union may bring benefits to all. Countries with higher social standards will not need to fear downward convergence, while countries that need to catch up can be confident that their economic development will be coupled with social development.

Progressive change in EU social policy is possible within the framework of the existing Treaty, but a more fundamental reform of economic governance necessitates new agreements among the member states. In the various fields where better functioning has required new tools or tighter coordination, progress has been possible even without a movement towards federalism. Financial and economic governance has been deepened in recent years, but this has to be followed up with more robust social governance and a focus on rights as well as outcomes. Popular support for a United States of Europe may be lacking, but with the right arguments, and sufficiently strong political alliances oriented towards the same objective, it can be built up in favour of a European social union.

References

Ágh, Attila. 1987. *Globális kihívás (Global Challenges)*. Budapest: Magvető Kiadó.

Alcidi, Cinzia, and Francesco Corti. 2020. Will SURE shield EU workers from the Corona crisis? *CEPS In Brief*, 6 April. URL: https://www.ceps.eu/will-sure-shield-eu-workers-from-the-corona-crisis.

Amable, Bruno. 2003. *The Diversity of Modern Capitalism*. Oxford: Oxford University Press.

Andor, László, and Martin Summers. 1998. *Market Failure: A Guide to the East European 'Economic Miracle'*. London: Pluto Press.

Andor, László. 2000. *Hungary on the Road to the European Union: Transition in Blue*. Westport, CT: Praeger Publishers, Greenwood Publishing Group.

Andor, László. 2013. *Erősödő Európa (Strengthening Europe)*. Budapest: Kossuth Kiadó.

Andor, László. 2017. *Jóléti modellek, európai válságok (Welfare Models, European Crises)*. Budapest: Noran Libro.

Andor, László. 2019. *Europa e solidarietà. Tra pilastro sociale e derive sovraniste*. Rome: Eurilink.

Andor, László. 2019. Fifteen years of convergence: east-west imbalance and what the EU should do about it. *Intereconomics* 54(1), 18–23.

Andor, László. 2021. A European Social Union. In *Our European Future: Charting a Progressive Course in the World*, edited by Maria João Rodrigues, pp. 63–68. London: London Publishing Partnership in association with the Foundation for European Progressive Studies.

Aranguiz, Ane. 2022. *Combating Poverty and Social Exclusion in European Union Law*. London: Routledge.

Armstrong, Stephen. 2018. *The New Poverty*. London: Verso.

Atkinson, Anthony B. 2015. *Inequality: What Can Be Done?* Cambridge, MA: Harvard University Press.

Avent, Ryan. 2017. *The Wealth of Humans: Work and Its Absence in the Twenty-First Century*. London: Penguin Books.

Banerjee, Abhijit V., and Esther Duflo. 2012. *Poor Economics: A Radical Rethinking of the Way to Fight Global Poverty*. New York: PublicAffairs.

Banerjee, Abhijit V., and Esther Duflo. 2019. *Good Economics for Hard Times*. New York: PublicAffairs.

Barr, Nicholas. 2020. *The Economics of the Welfare State*. Oxford: Oxford University Press.

Benanav, Aaron. 2020. *Automation and the Future of Work*. London: Verso.

Benifei, Brando. 2021. Artificial intelligence and social rights: a first assessment. *Progressive Post*, 7 May. URL: https://progressivepost.eu/artificial-intelligence-and-social-rights-a-first-assessment.

Boeri, Tito. 2015. Why we need a welfare union in Europe. *Social Europe*, 23 February 2015. URL: https://www.socialeurope.eu/welfare-union.

Boeri, Tito, and Juan Jimeno. 2016. Learning from the Great Divergence in unemployment in Europe during the crisis. *Labour Economics* 41, 32–46.

Bohle, Dorothee and Béla Greskovits. 2012. *Capitalist Diversity on Europe's Periphery*. Cornell Studies in Political Economy. Ithaca, NY: Cornell University Press.

Boltho, Andrea. 2020. Southern and Eastern Europe in the Eurozone: convergence or divergence? *Baltic Journal of Economics* 20(1), 74–93.

Bölükbasi, H. Tolga. 2021. *Euro-Austerity and Welfare States: Comparative Political Economy of Reform during the Maastricht Decade*. European Union Studies. Toronto: University of Toronto Press.

Brunnermeier, Markus, Harold James and Jean-Pierre Landau. 2016. *The Euro and the Battle of Ideas*. Princeton, NJ: Princeton University Press.

Bruzelius, Cecilia, and Martin Seeleib-Kaiser. 2017. European citizenship and social rights. In *A Handbook of European Social Policy*, edited by Patricia Kennett, Professor and Noemi Lendvai-Bainton, pp. 155-167. Cheltenham, UK: Edward Elgar Publishing.

Brynjolfsson, Erik, and Andrew McAfee. 2016. *The Second Machine Age: Work, Progress, and Prosperity in a Time of Brilliant Technologies*. New York: W.W. Norton & Company.

Budapest Institute for Policy Analysis. 2016. The impact of cohesion policy on corruption and political fovouritism. Report, August, Budapest Institute for Policy Analysis. URL: https://bit.ly/3RMufsE.

Cantillon, Bea, Martin Seeleib-Kaiser and Romke van der Veen. 2021. The COVID-19 crisis and policy responses by continental European welfare states. *Social Policy and Administration* 55(2), 326–338.

Case, Anne, and Angus Deaton. 2020. *Deaths of Despair and the Future of Capitalism.* Princeton, NJ: Princeton University Press.

Collier, Paul. 2015. *Exodus: How Migration is Changing Our World.* Oxford: Oxford University Press.

Corti, Francesco. 2022. *The Politicisation of Social Europe: Conflict Dynamics and Welfare Integration.* Cheltenham, UK: Edward Elgar Publishing.

Crespy, Amandine. 2022. *The European Social Question: Tackling Key Controversies.* New York: Agenda Publishing.

Crouch, Colin. 2020. *Social Europe: A Manifesto.* Berlin: Social Europe Publishing.

Csáki, György. 2009. *A látható kéz: A fejlesztő állam a globalizációban.* Budapest: Napvilág Kiadó.

Csáki, György, and Péter Farkas (eds). 2008. *A globalizáció és hatásai: Európai válaszok (Globalization and Its Effects: European Responses).* Budapest: Napvilág Kiadó.

Dauderstädt, Michael, and Cem Keltek. 2017. Inequality in Europe: relatively stable, absolutely alarming. Report, International Policy Analysis, Friedrich-Ebert-Stiftung, Berlin. URL: http://library.fes.de/pdf-files/id/ipa/13354.pdf.

Deaton, Angus. 2015. *The Great Escape: Health, Wealth, and the Origins of Inequality.* Princeton, NJ: Princeton University Press.

De Grauwe, Paul. 2016. *Economics of Monetary Union,* 11th edition. Oxford: Oxford University Press.

De la Porte, Caroline. 2021. Round table: from Lisbon to Porto; taking stock of developments in EU social policy; opening up the Pandora's box of EU social rights. *Transfer: European Review of Labour and Research* 27(4), 513–519.

Delors, Jacques. 2014. *Az új európai összhang (The New European Harmony).* Budapest: L'Harmattan Kiadó.

Dolvik, Jon Erik and Andrew Martin (eds). 2015. *European Social Models from Crisis to Crisis. Employment and Inequality in the Era of Monetary Integration.* Oxford: Oxford University Press.

Dorling, Danny. 2015. *Inequality and the 1%.* London: Verso.

Dullien, Sebastian. 2014. *A European Unemployment Benefit Scheme: How to Provide for More Stability in the Euro Zone.* Gütersloh, Germany: Verlag Bertelsmann Stiftung.

Dymarski, Wlodzimierz, Marica Frangakis and Jeremy Leaman (eds). 2014. *The Deepening Crisis of the European Union: The Case for Radical Change.* Poznań, Poland: Poznań University Press.

Eeckhout, Jan. 2021. *The Profit Paradox: How Thriving Firms Threaten the Future of Work.* Princeton, NJ: Princeton University Press.

El Khadraoui, Saïd. 2021. Green recovery: 'let's reimagine our future'. In *Progressive Yearbook 2021*, edited by Ania Skrzypek, pp. 55–65. Brussels: Foundation for European Progressive Studies.

Enderlein, Henrik, Lucas Guttenberg and Jann Spiess. 2013. *Blueprint for a Cyclical Shock Insurance in the Euro Area.* Report 100, September, Jacques Delors Institute.

Esping-Andersen, Gøsta. 1990. *The Three Worlds of Welfare Capitalism.* Cambridge: Polity Press.

European Commission. 2017. Reflection paper on harnessing globalisation. Reflection Paper, May, European Commission. URL: https://ec.europa .eu/info/publications/reflection-paper-harnessing-globalisation_en.

European Political Strategy Centre and the European Commission. 2016. The future of work: skills and resilience for a world of change. *EPSC Strategic Notes*, issue 13. URL: https://op.europa.eu/en/publicatio n-detail/-/publication/5236ecf2-ac93-11e6-aab7-01aa75ed71a1.

Evans, Eric J. 1997. *Thatcher and Thatcherism.* London: Routledge.

Ferge, Zsuzsa. 2017. *Magyar társadalom- és szociálpolitika (1990–2015) (Hungarian Social Policy, 1990–2015).* Budapest: Osiris.

Ferge, Zsuzsa, and Katalin Lévai (eds). 1991. *A jóléti állam (The Welfare State).* Budapest: ELTE.

Fernandes, Sofia. 2018. What is our ambition for the European Labour Authority? Policy Paper 219, March, Jacques Delors Institute. URL: https://www.hertie-school.org/en/delorscentre/publications/detail/ publication/what-ambition-for-the-european-labour-authority.

Ferrera, Maurizio (ed.). 2005. *Welfare State Reform in Southern Europe Fighting Poverty and Social Exclusion in Greece, Italy, Spain and Portugal.* London: Routledge.

Ferrera, Maurizio, Anton Hemerijck and Martin Rhodes. 2000. *The Future of Social Europe: Recasting Work and Welfare in the New Economy.* Oeiras, Portugal: Celta Editora.

Fischer, Georg, and Robert Strauss (eds). 2021. *Europe's Income, Wealth, Consumption, and Inequality*. Oxford: Oxford University Press.

Ford, Martin. 2016. *The Rise of the Robots: Technology and the Threat of Mass Unemployment*. London: Oneworld.

Forgács, Imre. 2015. *Az eltűnő munka nyomában: A Big Data és a pénztőke évszázada* (*On the Trail of Vanishing Labour: The Century of Big Data and Capital*). Budapest: Gondolat.

Freeman, Richard. 2015. The future of work: who owns the robot in your future work life? *Pacific Standard*, 17 August. URL: https://bit.ly/3D6zMWN.

Frey, Carl Benedikt. 2019. *The Technology Trap: Capital, Labor, and Power in the Age of Automation*. Princeton, NJ: Princeton University Press.

Frey, Carl Benedikt, and Michael A. Osborne. 2013. The future of employment: how susceptible are jobs to computerisation? *Technological Forecasting and Social Change* 114, 254–280.

Friedrichs, Günter, and Adam Schaff. 1984. *Mikroelektronika és társadalom: Áldás vagy átok* (*Microelectronics and Society: for Better or for Worse*). Budapest: Statisztikai Kiadó.

Galgóczi, Béla, Andrew Watt and Janine Leschke (eds). 2013. *EU Labour Migration since Enlargement: Trends, Impacts and Policies*. Farnham, UK: Ashgate.

Gamble, Andrew. 2009. *The Spectre at the Feast: Capitalist Crisis and the Politics of Recession*. London: Palgrave Macmillan.

Gamble, Andrew. 2014. *Crisis Without End? The Unravelling of Western Prosperity*. London: Palgrave Macmillan.

Garland, David. 2016. *The Welfare State: A Very Short Introduction*. Oxford: Oxford University Press.

Gerbaudo, Paolo. 2021. *The Great Recoil: Politics after Populism and Pandemic*. London: Verso.

Ghodsee, Kristen, and Mitchell Orenstein. 2021. *Taking Stock of Shock: Social Consequences of the 1989 Revolutions*. Oxford: Oxford University Press.

Giddens, Anthony. 2013. *Turbulent and Mighty Continent: What Future for Europe?* Cambridge: Polity Press.

Glyn, Andrew. 2006. *Capitalism Unleashed: Finance, Globalization and Welfare*. Oxford: Oxford University Press.

Habermas, Jürgen. 2013. *The Crisis of the European Union: A Response*. Cambridge: Polity Press.

Haggard, Stephan, and Robert R. Kaufman. 2020. *Development, Democracy, and Welfare States: Latin America, East Asia, and Eastern Europe.* Princeton, NJ: Princeton University Press.

Hassel, Anke, and Bruno Palier (eds). 2021. *Growth and Welfare in Advanced Capitalist Economies: How Have Growth Regimes Evolved?* Oxford: Oxford University Press.

Hay, Colin, and Daniel Wincott. 2012. *The Political Economy of European Welfare Capitalism.* London: Palgrave Macmillan.

Heimberger, Philipp. 2021. Die EU-Anleihen sind ein Zukunftsmodell für Europa. *Handelsblatt*, 8 January. URL: https://bit.ly/3AQkZgd.

Hemerijck, Anton. 2013. *Changing Welfare States.* Oxford: Oxford University Press.

Hemerijck, Anton, and Robin Huguenot-Noël. 2022. *Resilient Welfare States in the European Union.* New York: Agenda Publishing.

Hills, John. 2014. *Good Times, Bad Times: The Welfare Myth of Them and Us.* Bristol: Policy Press.

Huguenot-Noël, Robin, and László Andor. 2018. Balancing openness and protection: how can the EU budget help? Commentary Paper, 14 March, European Policy Centre.

Huws, Ursula. 2020. *Reinventing the Welfare State: Digital Platforms and Public Policies.* London: Pluto Press.

International Labour Organization. 2015. Guy Rider: anticipating the future of work essential for advancing social justice. *ILO Website*, 13 June. URL: https://www.ilo.org/ilc/ILCSessions/previous-sessions/104/WCMS_375766/lang--en/index.htm.

International Labour Organization. 2020. Covid-19 and the world of work. *ILO Website*. URL: https://www.ilo.org/global/topics/coronavirus/lang--en/index.htm.

Italianer, Alexander, and Jean Pisani-Ferry. 1994. The regional stabilisation properties of fiscal arrangements. In *Improving Economic and Social Cohesion in the European Community*, edited by Jørgen Mortensen. London: Palgrave Macmillan.

Klein, Steven. 2020. *The Work of Politics: Making a Democratic Welfare State.* Cambridge: Cambridge University Press.

Kornai, János. 1992. *The Socialist System: The Political Economy of Communism.* Oxford: Clarendon Press.

KPMG and GKI. 2017. A magyarországi európai uniós források felhasználásának és hatásainak elemzése a. 2007–2013 – as programozási időszak vonatkozásában. Report, March, KPMG and GKI. URL: https://bit.ly/3ql5lo9.

Laffan, Brigid and Alfredo De Feo (eds). 2020. *EU Financing for the Next Decade: Beyond the MFF 2021-2027 and the Next Generation EU*. Florence: European University Institute.

Lanier, Jaron. 2014. *Who Owns the Future?* New York: Simon & Schuster.

Lewis, Charles Paul. 2005. *How the East was Won: The Impact of Multinational Companies on Eastern Europe and the Former Soviet Union.* London: Palgrave Macmillan.

Lübker, Malte, and Thorsten Schulten. 2022. WSI minimum wage report 2022: towards a new minimum wage policy in Germany and Europe. Report, March, The Institute of Economic and Social Research (WSI).

Mahon, Rianne. 2011. The jobs strategy: from neo- to inclusive liberalism? *Review of International Political Economy* 18(5), 570–591.

Mazzucato, Mariana. 2018. *The Value of Everything: Making and Taking in the Global Economy.* London: Penguin Books.

McGaughey, Ewan. 2021. Will robots automate your job away? Full employment, basic income and economic democracy. *Industrial Law Journal* (https://doi.org/10.1093/indlaw/dwab010).

Merritt, Giles. 2016. *Slippery Slope: Europe's Troubled Future.* Oxford: Oxford University Press.

Milanović, Branko. 2005. *Worlds Apart: Measuring International and Global Inequality.* Princeton, NJ: Princeton University Press.

Milanović, Branko. 2010. *The Haves and the Have-Nots: A Brief and Idiosyncratic History of Global Inequality.* Princeton, NJ: Princeton University Press.

Mitchell, William. 2015. *Eurozone Dystopia: Groupthink and Denial on a Grand Scale.* Cheltenham, UK: Edward Elgar Publishing.

Morel, Nathalie, Bruno Palier and Joakim Palme (eds). 2012. *Towards a Social Investment Welfare State? Ideas, Policies and Challenges.* Bristol: Policy Press.

Morozov, Evgeny. 2014. *To Save Everything, Click Here: The Folly of Technological Solutionism.* New York: PublicAffairs.

Morozov, Evgeny. 2019. Digital socialism? The calculation debate in the age of Big Data. *New Left Review*, 116/117 (March/June).

Muldoon, James. 2022. *Platform Socialism: How to Reclaim our Digital Future from Big Tech*. London: Pluto Press.

Nathanson, Roby, and Itamar Gazala (eds). 2015. *Challenges for the Welfare State in the 21st Century: Insights from the 'Rebuilding the Welfare State in Multicultural Societies' Seminar*. Tel Aviv: Macro Center for Political Economics.

Nyilas, Mihály (ed.). 2009. *A jóléti állam a 21. században* (*The Welfare State in the 21st Century*). Budapest: Hilscher Rezső Szociálpolitikai Egyesület (Rezső Hilscher Association of Social Policy).

Ocampo, José Antonio, and Joseph E. Stiglitz (eds). 2018. *The Welfare State Revisited*. New York: Columbia University Press.

Odendahl, Christian. 2017. The Hartz myth: a closer look at Germany's labour market reforms. Policy Brief, July, Centre for European Reform.

Offe, Claus. 2015. *Europe Entrapped*. Cambridge: Polity Press.

Organisation for Economic Co-operation and Development. 2016.

Organisation for Economic Co-operation and Development. 2020. *OECD Employment Outlook 2020: Worker Security and the COVID-19 Crisis*. Paris: OECD Publishing.

Palier, Bruno (ed.). 2010. *A Long Goodbye to Bismarck? The Politics of Welfare Reform in Continental Europe*. Amsterdam: Amsterdam University Press.

Parker, Owen, and Dimitris Tsarouhas (eds). 2018. *Crisis in the Eurozone Periphery: The Political Economies of Greece, Spain, Ireland and Portugal*. London: Palgrave Macmillan.

Patomäki, Heikki. 2019. *Disintegrative Tendencies in Global Political Economy: Exits and Conflicts*. Rethinking Globalizations. London: Routledge.

Pennel, Denis. 2015. *The Ego Revolution at Work*. Paris: Works That Work.

Pettifor, Ann. 2019. *The Case for the Green New Deal*. London: Verso.

Phillips, Ben. 2020. *How to Fight Inequality (and Why that Fight Needs You)*. Cambridge: Polity Press.

Piatkowski, Marcin. 2018. *Europe's Growth Champion: Insights from the Economic Rise of Poland*. Oxford: Oxford University Press.

Pierson, Christopher. 1991. *Beyond the Welfare State?* Cambridge: Polity Press.

Pierson, Paul. 2010. *Dismantling the Welfare State? Reagan, Thatcher, and the Politics of Retrenchment*. Cambridge: Cambridge University Press.

Piketty, Thomas. 2014. *Capital in the Twenty-First Century*. Cambridge, MA: Belknap Press, Harvard University Press.

Polanyi, Karl. 2001. *The Great Transformation: The Political and Economic Origins of Our Time*. Boston, MA: Beacon Press.

Rayner, Laura. 2021. Rethinking EU economic governance: social investment. Policy Brief, 9 December, European Policy Centre. URL: https://www.epc.eu/en/Publications/Rethinking-EU-economic-governance-Social-investment-44b7cc.

Regan, Aidan. 2017. The imbalance of capitalisms in the Eurozone: can the north and south of Europe converge? *Comparative European Politics* 15(6), 969–990.

Rinaldi, David. 2016. A new start for social Europe. Report, Jacques Delors Institute.

Rodrigues, Maria João (ed.). 2021. *Our European Future: Charting a Progressive Course in the World*. London: London Publishing Partnership in association with the Foundation for European Progressive Studies.

Rodrik, Dani. 2012. *The Globalization Paradox: Democracy and the Future of the World Economy*. New York: W.W. Norton & Company.

Roszak, Theodore. 1986. *The Cult of Information: The Folklore of Computers and The True Art of Thinking*. New York: Pantheon.

Ryner, Magnus, and Alan Cafruny. 2017. *The European Union and Global Capitalism: Origins, Development, Crisis*. The European Union Series. London: Palgrave Macmillan.

Sachs, Jeffrey. 2006. *The End of Poverty: Economic Possibilities for Our Time*. London: Penguin Books.

Sandbu, Martin. 2020. *The Economics of Belonging: A Radical Plan to Win Back the Left Behind and Achieve Prosperity for All*. Princeton, NJ: Princeton University Press.

Sapir, André. 2006. Globalization and the reform of European social models. *Journal of Common Market Studies* 44(2), 369–390.

Saros, Daniel E. 2014. *Information Technology and Socialist Construction: The End of Capital and the Transition to Socialism*. London: Routledge.

Scharpf, Fritz. 2009. The double asymmetry of European integration: or, why the EU cannot be a social market economy. MPIfG Working Paper 09/12, Max Planck Institute for the Study of Societies.

Scheiring, Gábor. 2020. *The Retreat of Liberal Democracy: Authoritarian Capitalism and the Accumulative State in Hungary*. Challenges to Democracy in the 21st Century. London: Palgrave Macmillan.

Scheiring, Gábor, *et al.* 2021. Deindustrialization and the postsocialist mortality crisis. Working Paper 541, April, Political Economy Research Institute, University of Massachusetts Amherst.

Seikel, Daniel. 2021. The formula for a social Europe: complementary social policy plus a monetary union and internal market compatible with the European Social Model. Policy Brief 57, June, Institute of Economic Research (WSI).

Sissenich, Beate. 2007. *Building States without Society: European Union Enlargement and the Transfer of EU Social Policy to Poland and Hungary*. Washington, DC: Lexington Books.

Skrzypek, Ania (ed.). 2021. *Progressive Yearbook 2021*. Brussels: Foundation for European Progressive Studies.

Slobodian, Quinn. 2020. *Globalists: The End of Empire and the Birth of Neoliberalism*. Cambridge, MA: Harvard University Press.

Srnicek, Nick, and Alex Williams. 2015. *Inventing the Future: Postcapitalism and a World Without Work*. London: Verso.

Standing, Guy. 2011. *The Precariat: The New Dangerous Class*. London: Bloomsbury.

Stiglitz, Joseph E. 2002. *Globalization and Its Discontents*. New York: W.W. Norton & Company.

Stiglitz, Joseph E. 2012. *The Price of Inequality*. New York: W.W. Norton & Company.

Stiglitz, Joseph E. 2016. *The Euro: How a Common Currency Threatens the Future of Europe*. New York: W.W. Norton & Company.

Szalavetz, Andrea. 2009. A fejlesztő állam tudomány- és technológiapolitikája. In *A látható kéz: A fejlesztő állam a globalizációban*, edited by György Csáki. 2009. Budapest: Napvilág Kiadó.

Szamuely, László. 1985. *A jóléti állam ma (The Welfare State Today)*. Budapest: Magvető.

Szikra, Dorottya. 2018. Távolodás ez európai szociális modelltől: a szegénység társadalompolitikája (Moving away from the European social model: the social policy of poverty). *Magyar Tudomány*, 2018/6.

Therborn, Göran. 2013. *The Killing Fields of Inequality*. Cambridge: Polity Press.

Times of Malta. 2013. Grand coalition for digital jobs in the EU. *Times of Malta*, 14 March. URL: https://www.timesofmalta.com/articles/view/Grand-coalition-for-digital-jobs-in-the-EU.461478.

Timmins, Nicholas. 2017. *The Five Giants: A Biography of the Welfare State*. London: William Collins.

Tomka, Béla. 2008. *A jóléti állam Európában és Magyarországon (The Welfare State in Europe and Hungary)*. Budapest: Corvina.

Tooze, Adam. 2018. *Crashed: How a Decade of Financial Crises Changed the World*. London: Penguin Books.

Tooze, Adam. 2021. *Shutdown: How Covid Shook the World's Economy*. London: Penguin Books.

Vandenbroucke, Frank. 2020. We need a Europe that cares and that is seen to care. *Progressive Post*, 24 November. URL: https://progressivepost.eu/we-need-a-europe-that-cares-and-that-is-seen-to-care.

Vandenbroucke, Frank, Catherine Barnard and Geert De Baere (eds). 2017. *A European Social Union after the Crisis*. Cambridge: Cambridge University Press.

Vaughan-Whitehead, Daniel (ed). 2015. *The European Social Model in Crisis: Is Europe Losing Its Soul?* Cheltenham, UK: Edward Elgar Publishing.

Wilkinson, Richard, and Kate Pickett. 2009. *The Spirit Level: Why Equality Is Better for Everyone*. London: Bloomsbury.

Index